AF583288

I PROMISE TO PAY...

THE STORY OF PAPER CURRENCY IN INDIA

NAVIN BHATIA

INDIA • SINGAPORE • MALAYSIA

ISBN
Hardcase 979-8-89610-581-7
Paperback 979-8-89002-890-7

Cover picture:

> *The cover picture shows the symbol of the Indian Rupee and a collage of notes that are presently legal tender. These are in the denominations of ₹1, 2, 5, 10, 20, 50, 100, 200, 500 and 2,000. The ₹500 note is the most used note in circulation.*
>
> *As at the end of March 2024, the ₹500 note formed 41 per cent of the total volume (number of pieces) and 86.5 per cent of the total value of banknotes in circulation. (Source: RBI Annual Report 2023-24, p.155)*

Dedicated to

Lord Shri Rama,

with Whose Grace

this work could

be completed

Contents

Acknowledgement		7
Preface		9
Chapter One	Introduction	11
Chapter Two	The Early Years	23
Chapter Three	Central Bank Era	38
Chapter Four	Building Blocks	62
Chapter Five	Life Cycle	83
Chapter Six	Defective but Valued	99
Chapter Seven	Quest for Quality	116
Chapter Eight	Countering Counterfeits	132
Chapter Nine	Stripped of Value	148
Chapter Ten	Beyond Paper	164
Appendix I	*Governors of the Reserve Bank of India*	*179*
Appendix II	*Currency Management – Institutional Set-up*	*181*
Appendix III	*Salient Features of MG (New) Series of Notes*	*185*
Appendix IV	*Parameters for Payment of Mutilated Notes*	*192*
Appendix V	*Concept Note on Central Bank Digital Currency*	*193*
Endnotes		*196*

Acknowledgement

To the all-powerful and mighty search engine, Google, for providing smooth and easy access to the vast amount of reference material and data used in this work; the Reserve Bank of India, for providing me an opportunity to be involved in the management of currency, and thereby, getting to know about the life and times of paper currency so intimately; my former bosses, B.P.Vijayendra, formerly Principal Chief General Manager, Reserve Bank of India and Arnab Roy, formerly Principal Chief General Manager and Regional Director, Reserve Bank of India, for going through the draft and giving their valuable suggestions; my friends, Vijay Kumar Sharma, Suhas Joshi and Rajiv Kohli, for being there and encouraging me; and my better half, Anju and son, Mudit for going through multiple boring drafts and still having faith in my abilities as a writer!

Preface

During my postings in the Issue Department (the department dealing with matters related to currency) of the Reserve Bank of India, I got an opportunity to see the various facets of our paper currency very closely. The sight of hundreds of crates filled with bundles of crisp, crackling notes on the one hand and the limp, worn out, cut, torn, badly bruised, brittle and burnt notes on the other filled me with awe and wonder. I was also personally involved in performing the last rites of notes by burning them in huge incinerators decades ago as well as being witness to their automatic shredding and conversion into briquettes in the recent years. The experience was indeed poignant and humbling.

During the past few decades, there has been considerable mechanisation and automation in the area of handling of currency. This has rendered it possible to deal with the manifold increase in volumes of currency in the economy during this period. Although currency is handled by each and every one of us and is an integral part of our daily lives, yet very little is known to the public about its different aspects.

During my tenure in Issue Department, I had felt on several occasions that here was a story, waiting to be told. Paper currency - which, on the face of it, is just a piece of paper with a promise to pay written on it - was much more than that. Each and every piece of note had an exciting life of its own with all the challenges associated with it. My superannuation and the solitude induced by the lockdown during the pandemic led to the germination of the idea of putting what was in my mind to paper (or rather, on to the computer). The idea has now borne fruit in the form of this book.

I have attempted to narrate the life and times of paper currency in India right from its early beginnings in the late eighteenth century to the present times, when the Central Bank Digital Currency is being piloted by the Reserve Bank of India. This journey covers not only the significant changes that have taken place in our notes during this period but also several aspects such as, production, distribution, quality control, counterfeits, demonetisation and much more.

While the work is based on extensive research and references, it has been the endeavour to keep the language simple and interesting for the uninitiated reader. The more serious reader would also find the contents relevant to satisfy his or her curiosity and yearning for knowledge on the subject. Interesting nuggets of information have been highlighted in the text in exclusive boxes.

Yet, as the subject matter is sensitive, some aspects cannot be put into public domain. I have tried to give the complete picture, without compromising with the sensitivity of the subject.

I sincerely hope that that I have been modestly successful in my efforts to share the excitement that I have felt while dealing with notes. While all care has been taken to ensure that there are no errors of omission or commission, still if any shortcoming remains, the blame is entirely mine. Any suggestions for improvement would be welcome and be carried out in the forthcoming editions.

Navin Bhatia
Jaipur

Chapter One

Introduction

Why is there a need to tell the story of currency notes, we may well wonder? Currency notes are an important part of our daily lives, fulfilling our wants and facilitating our transactions. From birth to death, we have to deal with currency notes (or the lack of them!) while leading our day-to-day existence. Yet we take them for granted while knowing so little about them: where they are made, how they move through the economy and what happens to them when they become old and torn and how they are destroyed. Theirs is, indeed, a fascinating story, waiting to be told!

Currency notes come into our pockets or wallets, remain there for a few days and then move out to enter some others' pockets or wallets. They move from person to person, bank to bank or between ATMs (Automated Teller Machines) and people or banks innumerable times. Sometimes, they may remain bundled or stored for months or years in a locker or box. Sometimes, they may enter a bank's vault and remain there for days or months, only to come out again into the marketplace. They move through so many different abodes that indeed if they could speak, they would have many interesting tales to tell!

When needed, many of us get our currency notes from the ATMs and again deposit them back in the machines. Shopkeepers get currency notes from their customers, workers from their employers and borrowers from their lenders. Currency is indeed the lubricant which enables the financial transactions (and, therefore, the physical transactions) to be conducted smoothly within the economy. Some of us may handle currency notes with care and gentleness by not folding them. Others may not mind subjecting them to multiple folds and creases or even mistreating them by scribbling on them. We are all familiar with such instances in our daily transactions with currency notes. We make use of them while satisfying our wants for purchase of goods and services. But that's about all.

Most of us are so familiar with the form and appearance of currency notes that we do not even bother to read what is printed on them, and if at all, just their numerical value. In India, since our notes of different denominations have distinctly different colours and sizes, we may not even require reading the denominational value of the notes while using them. We just recognise them by their size and colour. Only when a new currency note comes into the market, we may evince interest in seeing it somewhat closely and commenting upon its size, colour, feature and design.

Yet, currency notes are important to all of us. Though they have become an integral part of our day-to-day lives, many may not know that paper currency, as we know it today, has just been around for less than two hundred years. Despite the increasing usage of debit and credit cards and electronic forms of money, for most of us, physical cash still accounts for the bulk of our transactions. As it is said, cash is still the king.

A few years ago, the interest in currency notes received a boost amongst the public when the two highest denomination notes were demonetised in 2016. This monetary event touched the lives of the entire population of the country because these notes were being used by almost everyone. Numerous questions on currency notes arose in the minds of the people and this event caught the attention, interest and curiosity of all of us, even the children. Again, in recent times, it is being said that currency notes would be consigned to history in the years to come and would be replaced by digital currency. So the curiosity about currency notes continues!

This story is an attempt to portray the life and times of currency notes in India. Since currency is a sensitive subject, some of its aspects are not available in public domain for public consumption. So, our story will capture, to the extent possible, how our currency notes have evolved over the years, how these are produced, how they move through the economy during their life span and some of the other interesting issues connected with them.

Although currency notes are part of our lives all the time, we do not stop to think about them. Like the air we breathe all the time but never think about its composition, its purity and how we should take care of it. Just like any other physical commodity, currency notes have to be produced, counted, packed and distributed (but no advertising is necessary!). This involves raw materials, machinery, packing and distribution channels. But unlike other commodities, currency notes have to be brought back after their useful life is over, again packed, counted, examined and ultimately destroyed. All these operations are performed silently, without publicity and under tight security so smoothly that we do not even come to know about them.

Many among us may know that the Reserve Bank of India is the entity which is responsible for currency in the country. Yes, it is true that the Reserve Bank of India plays a pivotal role in currency management. So much so that it has been considered as the *Brahma, Vishnu* and *Shiva* (the creator, protector and destroyer) of currency in the country, just as the trinity of the three Gods is considered to be the creator, protector and destroyer of life in Hindu religion.

The Promise to Pay

Though currency notes are mere pieces of printed paper, they carry value and are precious, in the sense that they empower the holder to exchange them with any goods or services. If we notice closely what is written on our currency notes, we will find the words 'I PROMISE TO PAY THE BEARER THE SUM OF...' written in capital letters, followed by the amount mentioned on the face of the notes. Thus, this piece of paper in our hands is a promise to pay the holder the amount of money indicated on it. This promise is made by none other than the Governor of the Reserve Bank of India on behalf of the Government of India. The signature appearing on the notes is that of the Governor of the Reserve Bank of India. (However, the one-rupee note is on a different footing; more about it later on.)

Promissory clause on a Fifty Rupee note

The promise to pay has been written on currency notes in India since their early days, though the language has changed over the years. While some early notes carried the phrase 'We promise to pay the bearer on demand...,' it was later changed to 'I promise to pay on demand...' The words 'on demand' which formed part of the promissory clause for long have since been dropped.

During the early days of paper currency, the promise implied that the issuer would pay the bearer, if demanded, the value of the sum mentioned on the note in metallic (silver) rupees. However, today the promise denotes the obligation on the part of the Reserve Bank of India towards the holder of the bank note.[1] It essentially implies that the note is legal tender for the amount mentioned thereon.

Prior to the Promise

As paper currency is of relatively recent origin, we may well wonder how goods and services were sold and purchased before the advent of currency notes. In the olden times, when people needed certain commodities which they did not have, they would exchange the commodities they possessed with what they needed. This system of exchange of goods or commodities is called the barter system. Barter is a system of exchange in which goods or services are directly exchanged for other goods or services without using a medium of exchange, such as money. In such a system, for example, a leather skin cloak could be exchanged for a spear, depending upon the need of the two parties.

The barter system had many limitations, which made the transactions very inefficient. Among them were: double coincidence of wants, implying that the needs of a seller of a commodity must match the needs of a buyer; absence of common measure of value; indivisibility of certain goods, which would not allow certain transactions to occur; and difficulty in storing wealth, especially of perishable goods.

Considering the difficulties involved in such a system, over time, barter got standardised in terms of metals or cowrie shells. Then, people knew the value of both the cloak and the spear, as in the above example, in terms of bronze or cowrie shells.[2] Over time, this evolved into metal currencies, with gold and silver being the most important. Metal currencies became the prevalent form of money for centuries. In India, various rulers had their own metal currencies in the form of coins.

The money system was a significant improvement over the barter system. It provided a way to quantify the value of goods and communicate it to others. Money has several defining characteristics: it is durable, divisible, portable, liquid (convertible), a unit of account, legal tender and difficult to counterfeit. As economists say, money is a medium of exchange, a unit of account and a store of value. It can be held and exchanged later for goods and services at an approximate value, and is also a standard of deferred payments.

The use of money as a medium of exchange removed the major difficulty of double coincidence of wants in the barter system. It separated the act of sale and purchase of goods and services and helped both parties in obtaining maximum satisfaction and profits independently. Money's most important usage is as a method of comparing the values of dissimilar objects.

Metal to Paper

The transition from metal currencies to paper money took a very long time. The first paper currency is reported to have started in China in the eleventh century in the form of promissory notes known as Jiaozi. These were initially used by private merchant enterprises and later became a recognised form of currency by local governments.

Ancient Chinese currency Jiaozi[3]

The Jiaozi were issued to replace the heavy coins that circulated in China at that time. Early Jiaozi were issued in high denominations; there were no standard denominations but were denominated according to the needs of the purchaser. The government office that issued these notes demanded a payment or exchange fee for exchanging coins with notes.[4]

Interestingly, in the thirteenth century, the European traveller, Marco Polo reported in his writings the description of paper money being used in China in the following words: All these pieces of paper are, issued with as much solemnity and authority as if they were of pure gold or silver... with these pieces of paper, made as I have described, Kublai Khan causes all payments on his own account to be made; and he makes them to pass current universally over all his kingdoms and provinces and territories, and whithersoever his power and sovereignty extends... and indeed everybody takes them readily, for wheresoever a person may go throughout the Great Khan's dominions he shall find these pieces of paper current, and shall be able to transact all sales and purchases of goods by means of them just as well as if they were coins of pure gold.[5]

However, it was only in the late seventeenth century when the first central banks were established in Sweden and England that the beginnings of paper currency can be said to have begun in the modern sense. In India, paper currency made a beginning in the late eighteenth century with note issues by some private banks.

Thus, money can take the form of either commodities (which have intrinsic value, such as gold or silver) or debt instruments. When money does not have intrinsic value, it must represent title to commodities that have intrinsic value or title to other debt instruments. In that respect, paper currency is representative money and essentially, a debt instrument. The owner of the currency knows who owes him or who has the underlying liability. There is always an 'issuer' of representative money.[6]

Money is usually issued by a sovereign. Private issuance of money has existed in the past but has over time given way to sovereign issuance, for two reasons. First, being a debt issuance, private money is only as good as the credit of the issuer. This makes private currency unstable as compared to sovereign currency. Second, paper currency involves seignorage, the difference between the intrinsic value and the representative value, which accrues to the issuer. This seignorage should accrue to the Government and not to any private individual.[7]

During the initial period, paper money was backed by metallic reserves in the form of gold and silver. The quantum of currency that could be issued by a country would be dependent upon the value of reserves it had in the form of gold or silver. However, modern paper currencies are essentially fiat currencies, in the sense that they may not be backed fully by metallic or other reserves.

In India, the then Government of India got the sole right to issue paper currency through the Paper Currency Act, 1861. After the Reserve Bank of India was established in 1935, it got the sole right to issue currency notes.

The notes issued by the Reserve Bank of India were initially backed by gold and sterling securities. Over time, the system has been revised to accommodate changing circumstances and provide flexibility. At present, the notes issued by Reserve Bank of India have a cent per cent cover in approved assets, comprising of gold coin and bullion, foreign securities and rupee securities. There is no ceiling on the amount of notes that can be issued by the Reserve Bank of India at any time.

Interestingly, although the Indian currency - like almost all currencies of the world - is a fiat currency in the sense that it cannot be exchanged for gold or silver by the holder from its issuer, how much gold does the Reserve Bank of India hold is a question that often comes to mind. As on March 31, 2024, the Reserve Bank of India held 822.10 metric tonnes of gold. Out of this, 308.03 metric tonnes was held in India as backing for the notes issued. The value of total gold held was ₹4,39,319.18 crore.[8]

Over the years, our currency notes have seen several changes in terms of their sizes, colours and designs. The text mentioned on the notes, its language, the motifs and designs used on the obverse as well as reverse have all changed, reflecting the changing times that the country has gone through. The denominations in which currency notes have been printed have also not remained the same. While some denominations have been gone out of existence, other newer ones have been added. A few denominations have been discontinued in the past, only to be reintroduced some years later.

Currency Notes and Banknotes or Bank Notes

Strictly speaking, the term currency notes refers to notes issued by the Government of India, which are the one-rupee notes. As all other notes are issued by the Reserve Bank of India, these are called banknotes. But in popular parlance, when the term currency notes is used, it is considered to mean all denomination of notes. In the present story, the term 'currency notes' has been used in the popular sense of the term. However, wherever the term 'banknotes' or 'bank notes' is used, it refers to the notes issued by the Reserve Bank of India, that is, all notes except the one-rupee notes.

The one-rupee currency note is essentially a one-rupee coin, in the form of a paper note. That's why the one-rupee coin is depicted prominently on the face of the one-rupee note. The one-rupee note does not contain the promissory clause 'I promise to pay the bearer' and also does not carry the signature of the Governor of the Reserve Bank of India. Instead, it bears the signature of the Finance Secretary of the Government of India. This note has its origin in the period of the First World War, when it was first introduced to conserve the metal for the one-rupee coin. It has been discontinued more than once, only to be reintroduced again.

Threat to Paper

The sovereignty enjoyed by paper currency for well over a century is now being threatened by new forms of money. While credit and debit cards and electronic wallets have tried to dent the usage of paper currency in the last few decades, these were not able to make much impact. However, the emergence of cryptocurrencies has made the central banks all over the world sit up and take notice. Many countries are now in the process of designing their own Central Bank Digital Currencies (CBDCs).

Despite India having already announced the launch of its CBDC during 2022-23, it may yet take some years for it to be adopted on a large scale. At the global level too, CBDCs are still in the formative stage. As things stand, it may still be too early to write the epitaph of paper currency in India.

How This Story Unfolds

In the pages that follow, this story tries to capture some important and interesting facets of paper currency in India. It begins with the most familiar aspects of currency notes, their appearance and design, and how these have changed over time. We know that now the Reserve Bank of India is the issuing authority for currency notes in the country. But it was not always so, as paper currency came into existence much before the Reserve Bank of India was established in 1935. The major features of currency notes, before and after the Reserve Bank of India came into being, are covered in the first two separate chapters.

The requirement of currency notes as well as the infrastructure required for producing them, such as printing presses, paper and ink and how it has developed over time is the subject matter of the next chapter. It also describes the various security features that are embedded in our currency notes. Once the currency notes are produced, these are supplied to the Reserve Bank of India for being put into circulation in the economy. Our story moves on to narrate the life cycle of the currency notes from their youth to old age and ultimate death (destruction).

During handling in the course of their life span, some currency notes may get soiled or develop tears or some portions may get missing. The system of obtaining value of such defective currency notes is covered next. In order to maintain the quality of currency notes in the economy, the Reserve Bank of India has been taking several initiatives under its Clean Note Policy, particularly over the last over two decades. The story moves on to describe these measures, which have helped improve the quality of currency in the country.

The attraction of producing counterfeit notes resembling the real currency has existed ever since paper currency came into existence. The challenge of dealing with counterfeit notes is described next. The story then moves on to describe the occasions when the legal tender accorded to certain higher denomination notes was withdrawn. This measure, called demonetisation, has been taken thrice so far to curb black or illegal money.

And finally, the story paints the scenario of new forms of currency which have the power and potential to determine the future of paper currency. These include, credit and debit cards, electronic wallets, cryptocurrency and, finally, the Central Bank Digital Currency.

As you set out on this journey of discovery of the story of paper currency, here's wishing you, *Bon Voyage!*

Chapter Two

The Early Years

The story of paper currency in India begins in the late eighteenth century, when many parts of India were under the rule of the British East India Company. It was during that period when the first paper currency notes were issued by some of the private banks of those times. However, these notes had limited circulation and were confined to limited geographical jurisdiction. Through the Paper Currency Act, 1861 the then Government of India got the sole power to issue currency notes. For over seven decades, the note issue function remained with the Government of India, till the formation of the Reserve Bank of India in 1935. This chapter narrates in brief the story of paper currency notes issued by private banks as well as the then Government of India during this period. It also touches upon the currency notes issued in those territories which were not under the British rule.

During the hundred years between 1757 and 1857, the British East India Company was transformed from a trading company to a territorial colonial power. It gradually acquired sovereignty over large parts of India, especially in the eastern, southern and western parts of the country. By 1857, it came to exercise direct rule over about 63 per cent of the territory and 78 per cent of the population of the Indian subcontinent. The mutiny of 1857 was a turning point in the history of India as it led to the enactment of the Government of India Act,

1858 by which the British East India Company was dissolved and its functions transferred to the British Crown.

Paper currency, in the modern sense, evolved in India during the rule of the British East India Company. The earliest paper currency notes were issued by some of the private banks. These banks were primarily located at the important trading centres of Calcutta (now Kolkata), Bombay (now Mumbai) and Madras (now Chennai).

'Free Banking Era'

Prior to 1861, paper currency notes were not governed by any central legislation. This period could be alluded to as the 'Free Banking Era' in India. It was the time when banks in India were not only free to issue cheques but also free to issue promissory notes, which were payable to bearer on demand. Thus, these promissory notes had the character of currency notes and were also referred to as bank notes. These notes were convertible on demand to current coins of the region.[9]

The words used on the face of early notes of this period were 'We promise to pay to ... or Bearer on demand the sum of Rupees ...' The promise clause was amended in later years to omit the name of the payee and read 'I promise to pay the bearer on demand...'

The Bank of Hindostan and the General Bank in Bengal and Bihar were among the earliest to issue notes. The Bank of Hindostan was set up in 1770 by the agency house of Alexander and Company. It survived three panic runs only to collapse during a commercial crisis in 1832.[10] The circulation of its notes, denominated in Sicca Rupees, the currency of British East India Company, was confined to Calcutta and the immediate neighbourhood. The Government refused to confer on the notes the standing of legal tender money and did not accept them in any of its Treasuries.[11]

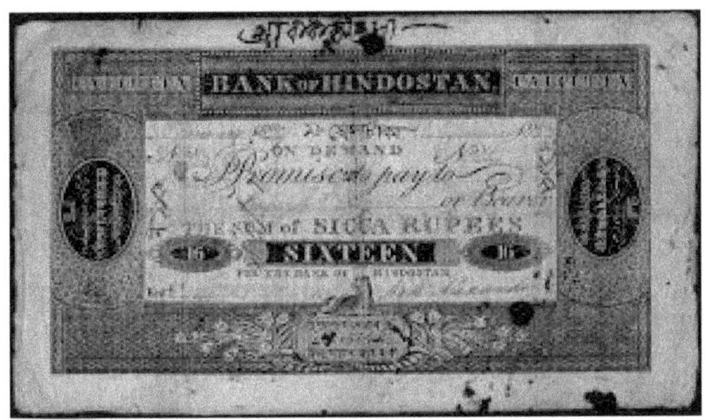

A Bank of Hindostan Sicca Rupees Sixteen note, among the earliest notes to be issued[12]

The General Bank in Bengal and Behar was set up in 1773 as a state sponsored institution. Its government backing ensured it was successful and profitable and its notes enjoyed government patronage. However, it was wound up in 1775. The other banks in the eastern region which issued their own notes were The Bengal Bank (1784-91), the Commercial Bank (1819-28), the Calcutta Bank (1824-29) and the Union Bank (1829-48).

In western India, the Oriental Banking Corporation (1842-1884) and the Commercial Bank of India (1845-66) were among the banks which issued their notes. Notes of the Oriental Banking Corporation featured the Town Hall of Bombay as a vignette. This bank also issued notes in Ceylon (now Sri Lanka). The Commercial Bank of India issued exotic notes with an inter-blend of western and eastern motifs.

In southern India, the Government Bank (1806-43) is also referred to among the note issuing banks. However, strictly speaking, the so called notes of this bank were more in the nature of treasury bills by which the government raised funds at that time.

Three Presidency Banks

Official patronage was an important factor in the acceptance of currency notes. That is why with the setting up of Presidency Banks, which were semi-Government in nature, and which issued their own notes, the use of notes gained importance. The first Presidency Bank to be set up was the Bank of Bengal in 1806, initially called the Bank of Calcutta. It was established by a Government Charter with a capital of 50 lakh (5 million) Sicca Rupees, the currency of the British East India Company. The Charter gave the bank the privilege to issue notes for circulation within its circle. The Charter also required the bank to maintain cash reserves and provided limits to note issue.

Early notes issued by the Bank of Bengal were unifaced (printed on one side) and denominated in Sicca Rupees as well as gold mohurs.[13] These are referred to as the Unifaced Series. Subsequent issues were printed on both sides. These carried the picture of a female figure, personifying 'commerce'. These notes are referred to as the Commerce Series. After 1835, the notes were issued in Company Rupees instead of Sicca Rupees.[14] The denominations were in Rs 10, 15, 16, 20, 25, 50, 100, 250, 500, 1000 and 10,000.[15] The name of the bank and the denomination was written on the notes in three languages, namely, Bengali, Nagri (Hindi) and Urdu.

Around 1856, due to technological developments and security considerations, the design of notes was changed to include intricate patterns and multiple colours. The 'commerce' motif was replaced by 'Britannia' motif to convey the grandeur of the British Empire. These notes are referred to as the Britannia Series. By 1861, the total value of the notes of Bank of Bengal in circulation was about Rs 177 lakh (Rs 17.7 million)[16], the highest among the three Presidency Banks.

The second Presidency Bank was established in Bombay (now Mumbai) in 1840 with a capital of Rs 52.25 lakh (Rs 5.22 million). Called the Bank of Bombay, it had a number of Indians as directors, including Framji Cowasji Banaji, Jamshedji Jeejeebhoy and Seth Premchund Roychund. The notes issued by the Bank of Bombay carried the vignettes of the Town Hall and also the statues of Mountstuart Elphinstone and John Malcom, both former Governors of Bombay.

Around 1861, the value of notes in circulation of the Bank of Bombay was about Rs 100 lakh (Rs 10 million)[17].

A Bank of Bombay Rupees Ten note featuring Mountstuart Elphinstone and John Malcom[18]

The third Presidency Bank, the Bank of Madras, was established in 1843 with a capital of Rs 30 lakh (Rs 3 million). It replaced the Government Bank, which had earlier been set up in 1806. The notes issued by this bank bore the vignette of Sir Thomas Munroe, who was Governor of Madras from 1817-27. Among the Presidency banks, the Bank of Madras had the smallest issue of banknotes. The value of circulation of its notes in 1860 was only Rs 24.5 lakh (Rs 2.45 million).

Incidentally, the three Presidency Banks (which lost their note issuing powers with the promulgation of the Paper Currency Act, 1861) were amalgamated to form the Imperial Bank of India in 1921.

Paper Currency Act, 1861

With the enactment of the Paper Currency Act, 1861 (Act XIX of 1861), the then Government of India got the sole right to issue banknotes in India, bringing to an end the issuance of bank notes by various banks. On March 1, 1862, the Department of Issue of Paper Currency was set up. It was later referred to as Paper Currency Department or Currency Department. It was part of the Finance Department of the British Government, whose head was the Finance Member of the Indian colonial administration. The three major note-issuing banks, the Bank of Bengal, Bank of Bombay, and Bank of Madras, which were all partly government-owned at the time, were compensated for the loss of their note issues by being made the agents for the government note issue until 1866, when the Paper Currency Department was ready to do the work on its own.[19]

The Paper Currency Act, 1861 initially divided India into three Currency Circles, namely, Calcutta, Bombay and Madras with each Circle issuing its own notes. The notes were legal tender only in the respective Circle in which these were issued. However, payment of dues to the Government could be made in notes of any Currency Circle.

The Paper Currency Act, 1861 stipulated that Rupees Ten would be the minimum denomination of notes that could be issued. This was a rather high denomination of note considering the purchasing power at that time.

The first set of British India notes issued after the commencement of the Paper Currency Act, 1861 are referred to as the 'Victoria Portrait Series' notes as they carried a small portrait of Queen Victoria on the top left. These notes were issued in denominations of Rs 10, 20, 50, 100 and 1000. These notes were unifaced and printed on hand-moulded paper manufactured at the Laverstock Paper Mills aka Portals (which had been making paper for Bank of England notes since 1727). The security features incorporated the watermark (GOVERNMENT OF INDIA, RUPEES, two signatures and wavy lines), printed signature and registration of notes.[20]

A Government of India Rupees Ten note Queen Victoria Series (1865)[21]

The 'Victoria Portrait Series' of notes had, however, to be withdrawn in 1867 in wake of large number of forgeries. These notes were replaced by the 'Unifaced Underprint Series' of notes, with improved security features. The wavy line watermark now included a manufacturer's code. These notes carried a green coloured underprint, guilloche (geometric lathe) patterns and, initially, four language panels. Subsequently, the green underprint was replaced by red underprint and eight language panels.

In 1871, the Paper Currency Act was amended to bring down the minimum value of notes that could be issued to Rupees Five. Consequently, notes in the Rupees Five denomination were issued that year.

Since these were all high denomination notes at that time, these were rarely used by the general public. In his book, 'History of Indian Currency & Banking', Dr B.R. Ambedkar has remarked, "In a country where the average range of transactions did not exceed Rs 1 and were as low as 1 anna or even lower, it is impossible to expect that paper currency could, to any great extent, figure in the dealings of the people. Even Rs 5 notes were not low enough to penetrate into the economic life of the people."[22]

Rather, these were used largely for collection of revenue and remittance of funds for commercial and official purposes. Most transactions by common people were done in coins. Coin circulation likely exceeded note circulation during this period. In March 1900, for instance, note circulation was 287 million rupees, while estimated coin circulation exceeded one billion rupees. As the Paper Currency Department Annual Report, 1902 stated, "Except in the near neighbourhood of the chief centres of trade, Currency Notes are hardly at all in circulation, partly because the common transactions of people in towns and villages are on too small a scale for a high-value currency, and partly because Government cannot undertake to encash Notes at every Treasury".[23]

The restrictive nature of Currency Circles was gradually relaxed between 1903 and 1911. By that time, notes in the 5, 10, 50 and 100 denominations had been universalised, that is, were acceptable in Currency Circles other than in which these were issued. The number of Currency Circles was raised to seven in 1910 with the addition of Cawnpore (Kanpur), Karachi, Lahore and Rangoon (Yangon) to the existing three.

Interestingly, in those days, when money had to be securely transferred across distances, the paper notes were sometimes cut in half, with one half being sent by post first and the second sent only after the first reached the destination. At the receiving end, the receiver would then paste the two pieces and claim value. Following the payment, the note was marked as 'cancelled' and the signature portion torn to prevent reuse. The note was retained, but only for accounting purposes.[24]

The First World War was instrumental in introducing lower denomination notes as the price of silver rose sharply and the rupee was becoming worth more as metal than as money. In 1917, the One Rupee note was introduced, followed by the Rupees Two and Annas Eight note a year later. The One Rupee note depicted a silver coin image of King George V, who had taken over as Emperor in 1910. The issuance of these notes was discontinued less than ten years later, in 1926, on cost benefit considerations.[25]

Interestingly, the value of the exotic Rupees Two and Annas Eight notes released on January 2, 1918 was the exact equivalent of $1 at the time. These notes bore the emblem of King George V and the signature of erstwhile British Finance Secretary M.M.S. Gubbay. The notes were numbered by seven prefix code variations denoting their circle of issue: A (Cawnpore), B (Bombay), C (Calcutta), K (Karachi), L (Lahore), M (Madras) and R (Rangoon). The value ('adhai rupya') was stated at the back in eight Indian languages. In the beginning, the notes did not evoke trust among the people, and were used in the market only at a discount of 15 - 19 per cent. They were only accepted at par after about a year or two passed since they were introduced into circulation. Today, these notes are a collector's delight. A surviving currency note was auctioned for a hammer price Rs 640,000 in Mumbai's Todywalla auctions on December 2, 2015.[26]

A Government of India Rupees Two Annas Eight note of King's Portrait series[27]

The portrait of King George V was used on Rupee Ten notes in 1923 and subsequently in notes of all denominations. These notes came to be called 'King's Portrait Series' and gradually replaced the 'Unifaced

Underprint Series'. The King's portrait motif continued as an integral feature on all subsequent paper money issues of British India.[28]

The notes issued during this period were printed in England. It was only in 1925 when a Security Press was set up in India followed by the Currency Note Press in 1928. Both were located at Nasik (now Nashik) in western India (now in Maharashtra). Printing of currency notes in India started in 1928. Improved security features for these notes included a clear watermark window, intricate portraits of the King, and multi-coloured printing.[29]

The paper currency system during this period was based on the principle that the number of notes printed, and their total amount, could change only with the variation on metallic reserves apart from limited fiduciary limits against government securities.

The Paper Currency Act, 1861 provided for issue of notes on demand in exchange for Indian silver rupees, silver bullion, or foreign silver coin evaluated at its bullion value, and to redeem notes in silver. The Government could also provide for the Paper Currency Department to accept gold at specified rates. Initially, the Department could hold up to 40 million rupees of Indian government securities but had to back any rupees in circulation in excess of that amount 100 per cent with precious metals. The limit of 40 million rupees was revised upward on five occasions to 140 million rupees in 1911, of which up to 40 million could be British government securities.[30]

As the magnitude of note issue increased, the Paper Currency Department was made independent and the Office of the Controller of Currency was created in 1913. The department continued to issue notes until the Reserve Bank of India was set up in 1935.

Notes of Princely States

During that period, and even later on, the entire India was not under British rule. There were numerous princely states in existence. While some princely states issued their own coins, the British strongly discouraged them from issuing their own notes. Only two princely states had issued paper currency, namely, Jammu & Kashmir in 1876 and Hyderabad, commencing from 1918. While the Government of Kutch had prepared specimens of currency notes, these were not issued.[31]

The currency notes of the state of Jammu & Kashmir were used only for payment to the state treasuries of land revenue and other government dues. The denominations ranged from one rupee to one thousand rupees. These were all dated *Samvat* 1934 (1877 AD). These carried the 'Sun' motif of the Dogra family. The central panel carried the inscription in Nagari: "Shrikar" (meaning *Sarkar* or Government). The numeral value was given in Persian, Nagari and Dogri (languages). The notes were printed at Vidyavilas Press, Jammu.[32]

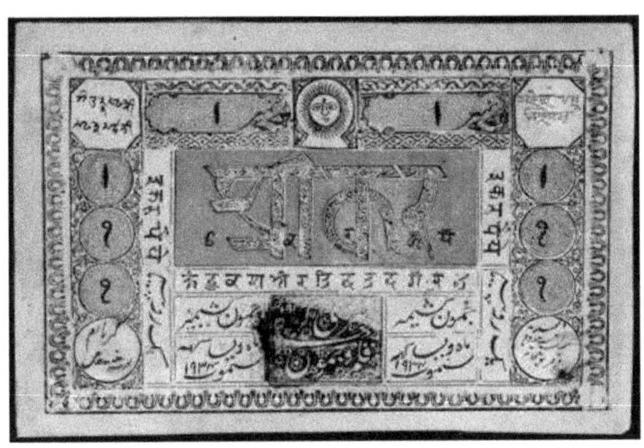

A Jammu & Kashmir One Rupee note, carrying the inscription 'Shrikar' and the Sun motif[33]

Due to shortage of silver and coins during the First World War, in 1918, the British Government allowed the princely State of Hyderabad to issue its own paper currency. These were called the 'Osmania Sicca Rupee' notes printed in Urdu and initially issued in denominations of Rupees 10 and 100. The Rupee One and Five denominations were issued in 1919 while Rupees 1,000 notes were issued in 1926. These notes were primarily Islamic in character and bore no pictures. These were dated in 'Fasli' years, an era which was current in the Deccan, associated closely with the Hijri era. The notes were printed by Messrs Waterlow and Sons, London. After the Currency Note Press was set up at Nasik, the notes of the State of Hyderabad were printed there for reasons of economy and security. These notes were issued up to 1953 and were demonetised in 1959, although the State had acceded to the Indian Union in 1948.

An Osmania Sicca Rupees Five note[34]

During the Second World War, there was an acute scarcity of small coins throughout India. During this period, several small princely states in Western India like Bikaner and Bundi (now in Rajasthan) and Junagadh, Morvi and Rajkot (now in Gujarat) issued what are alluded to as Cash Coupons to meet the shortage. Most Cash Coupons were printed crudely on press board. Their place in the history of Indian Paper Money is in the realm of exigent money (emergency issues).[35]

Portuguese and French Notes

During this period, apart from the British, the Portuguese and French also controlled certain territories in India. The Portuguese ruled over Goa, Daman, Diu and Dadra and Nagar Haveli. In 1883, the Public Finance Department of the Portuguese government began issuing paper currency in India in the form of 'Rupia' denominated notes.

These were issued in denominations of 5, 10, 20, 50, 100 and 500. However, no specimen of these notes has survived. The notes issued in a later series carried the portrait of the King of Portugal.

In 1906, Banco Nacional Ultramarino was entrusted with the responsibility of issue of paper money in India for the Portuguese held territories. The early notes issued by the bank carried the seal of the bank.[36] In 1917, new denominations of 4 Tangas, 8 Tangas and One Rupia and Two and a Half Rupias were issued. M/s Bradbury & Wilkinson of London printed all these paper currencies.[37]

As per the Portuguese system, one Rupia consisted of 16 Tangas, corresponding to *annas*. Most of these issues carried the Commerce and Sailing Ships motifs common to many colonial issues. Indian symbols and motifs (architectural and exotic fauna) were adopted on some notes. Later notes carried the portrait of Afonso De Albuquerque. It has been brought out that some issues of One Rupia and the Two and a Half Rupia notes depicted the famous Jagannath temple of Puri on the reverse.[38]

In 1959, the denominational unit was changed from Rupia to Escudos with one Escudo consisting of 100 Cent avos. New notes with the denominations of 30, 60, 100, 300, 600 and 1000 Escudos were introduced. These remained in circulation till 1961, when Goa was annexed to the Indian Union.[39]

An Oito Tanga note (One half of a Rupia) issued by Banco Nacional Ultramarino (1917)[40]

The French territories in India included Pondicherry, Karaikal, Mahe, Yanam and Chandernagore. In 1898, France's Banque de l'Indochine issued its own 'Roupie' notes for the French territories in India. The Roupie consisted of eight Fanons and one Fanon was equivalent to two annas. These notes were in the denomination of 10 and 50. Notes of One Roupie were issued after the First World War.

A Rupee One note issued by Banque De L'Indochine (1938) for the French territories in India[41]

New notes of 50 Roupies carried the bust of Dupleix, who founded the French Empire in India. These notes continued to be in circulation till they were replaced by Indian currency in 1954[42], with the transfer of Pondicherry and other territories to India.

Endnote

Paper currency in India had a modest beginning in limited geographies with limited circulation and multiple issuers. Over the years, it grew in importance and got legal recognition. Gradually, all financial transactions shifted from metallic currency to paper currency. The then Government of India exercised full control over paper currency for over seven decades, from 1861 to 1935.

The next part of our story will begin with briefly exploring how the Reserve Bank of India was set up and took over the function of issuing of notes from the then Government of India. It will then narrate the highlights of the notes issued by the Reserve Bank of India since inception till the present times. It is, indeed, a fascinating tale, depicting the major changes which have come about in the Indian currency over a period of over eight decades in tune with the changing times.

Chapter Three

Central Bank Era

Monday, the first of April, 1935 is a landmark day in the story of currency notes in India. It was the day the Reserve Bank of India was formed and took over the function of note issue and management from the then Government of India. Starting as a private shareholders bank, it was nationalised in 1949. As the central bank of the country, the Reserve Bank of India has been entrusted with the authority to issue bank notes of various denominations. This part of the story narrates the genesis of the Reserve Bank of India and the legal backing it has to perform the functions of note issue. It further describes the main features of the various currency notes issued since then and how these have evolved and changed over the years.

As mentioned earlier, the three Presidency Banks (Bank of Bombay, Bank of Bengal and Bank of Madras) were amalgamated to form the Imperial Bank of India in 1921. This bank was primarily a commercial bank. However, it was entrusted with certain central banking functions such as being the sole banker to the Government of India as well as managing its public debt. The note issuing function continued with the Government of India.

Earlier, in 1920, the International Financial Conference held at Brussels had passed a resolution to the effect that 'in countries where there is no central bank of issue, one should be established'. In 1922, the second Conference convened at Genoa also made a similar recommendation. Since then, several countries set up central banks, like South Africa (1921), Colombia (1923), and Hungary and Poland (1924).[43]

Hilton Young Commission

In 1925, the Royal Commission on Indian Currency and Finance (popularly known as Hilton Young Commission) was appointed 'to examine and report on the Indian exchange and currency system and practice; to consider whether any modifications are desirable in the interests of India and to make recommendations'. The question of setting up a central bank was not specifically referred to it. The Commission, however, examined this matter and in its Report, submitted in July 1926, strongly recommended the establishment of a central bank. The bank was to be called the 'Reserve Bank of India', and all central banking functions were to be entrusted to it.[44]

Pointing out the inherent weakness of the Indian system at that time, where the control of currency and credit was in the hands of two different authorities, the Commission remarked, "The Government controls the currency. The credit situation is controlled, as far as it is controlled at all, by the Imperial Bank. With divided control, there is likelihood of divided counsels and failure to co-ordinate...The only certain way to secure coordination is to concentrate the controls in one hand. In other countries the single controlling hand is that of a Central Bank."[45] The Commission recommended that Reserve Bank should be a shareholders' Bank, with a paid-up capital of Rs. 5 crore and provided details about its management.

Consequently, a Bill to set up a central bank was introduced in the Legislative Assembly in 1927. The Bill had provisions for private capital and restrictions on political appointees to preserve the institution's independence. It was referred to a Joint Committee where it did not have a smooth sailing. Within the Committee, there were irreconcilable differences related to the ownership of the Bank as well as its constitution and composition of its Board of Directors.

An amended version of the Bill was introduced in 1928. During this period, the Bill was taken up for consideration twice and on both occasions it was decided to postpone further consideration after some clauses/sub-clauses had been approved. Ultimately, the Bill was dropped.

In 1931, the issue regarding the establishment of the Bank was revived on the recommendations of the Indian Central Banking Enquiry Committee. This Committee strongly recommended the establishment of a Reserve Bank 'at the earliest possible date'. In the meanwhile, a Departmental Committee was appointed in London by the India Office to advise regarding the nature of Reserve Bank legislation. The Committee, in its Report of 1933, strongly recommended a shareholders' bank, observing that 'State capital, however safeguarded, is a direct incentive to political interference'.[46]

The India Office Committee's Report was followed up by the appointment in London of another committee to prepare draft legislation. The Reserve Bank of India Bill, 1933, drafted on the basis of the recommendations of the London Committee, was introduced in the Legislative Assembly in September, 1933.

In his speech introducing the Bill, the Finance Member explained the significance of a Reserve Bank in the constitutional plan as follows:

"It has generally been agreed in all the constitutional discussions, and the experience of all other countries bears this out, that when the direction of public finance is in the hands of a ministry responsible to a popularly elected Legislature, a ministry which would for that reason be liable to frequent change with the changing political situation, it is desirable that the control of currency and credit in the country should be in the hands of an independent authority which can act with continuity... Further, the experience of all countries is again united in leading to the conclusion that the best and indeed the only practical device for securing this independence and continuity is to set up a Central Bank, independent of political influence."[47]

The Bill was referred to a Joint Select Committee and, as amended by the Committee, was introduced in the Legislative Assembly in November, 1933 at a special session. This session was not attended by the Congress party, which had vigorously championed the principle of State ownership of the proposed Reserve Bank, when the 1927 Bill had come up before the Legislature. The Bill was passed by the Assembly in December, 1933 and by the Council of State in February, 1934. The Bill received the assent of the Governor-General in March, 1934.

Reserve Bank of India is Formed

The Reserve Bank of India was formally inaugurated on Monday, April 1, 1935, the first day of the fiscal year with an initial share capital of Rupees Five crore (Rupees 50 million). The share capital has remained unchanged till date. The headquarters of the Reserve Bank of India was initially located at Calcutta (now Kolkata) but was shifted to Bombay (now Mumbai) in December, 1937, where it has remained ever since. In 1979, the headquarters, called Central Office, shifted to its new building, on Shahid Bhagat Singh Marg in South Mumbai.

Sir Osborne A. Smith, an Australian by birth, who was serving as one of the two Managing Governors of Imperial Bank of India, was appointed the first Governor of the Reserve Bank of India with a term of office of three and a half years.[48] A complete list of Governors of the Reserve Bank of India along with their tenures is given in Appendix I.

Interestingly, while deciding the seal (logo) of the Reserve Bank of India, the general ideas were that it should emphasise the Governmental status of the Bank, but not too closely; it should have something Indian in the design; it should be simple, artistic and heraldically correct; and the design should be such that it could be used without substantial alteration for letter heading, etc. For this purpose, various seals, medals and coins were examined. The East India Company Double Mohur, with the sketch of the Lion and Palm Tree, was found most suitable; however, it was decided to replace the lion by the tiger, the latter being regarded as the more characteristic animal of India![49] The Reserve Bank's seal appears on the obverse (front) of all bank notes. During the earlier years, it used to appear on the reverse of the notes. The present design is also slightly different from the design used in the initial years. The name 'Reserve Bank of India' now appears in both Hindi and English as against only in English during the earlier years.

Seal of the Reserve Bank of India, which appears on all bank notes

Legal Framework for Note Issue

The Reserve Bank of India Act, 1934 transferred the power to issue currency notes and management of currency in India from the then Government of India to the Reserve Bank of India. The broad legal framework governing the issuance of notes by the Bank provides that:

- the Bank has the sole right to issue bank notes in India and also issue currency notes of the Government of India (Section 22);
- the issue of notes shall be conducted by the Bank in an Issue Department which shall be separated and kept wholly distinct from the Banking Department (Section 23);
- the bank notes can be in the denomination of values of Rupees 2, 5, 10, 20, 50, 100, 500 1,000, 5,000 and 10,000 or of such other denominational values, not exceeding Rupees

10,000, as may be specified by the Central Government on the recommendation of the Central Board (Section 24); and

- the design, form and material of bank notes shall be such as may be approved by the Central Government after consideration of the recommendations made by Central Board (Section 25).

The department within the Reserve Bank of India that deals with currency is the Department of Currency Management. Within the Government of India, the Coin and Currency Division in the Department of Economic Affairs under the Ministry of Finance deals with currency related matters. The broad areas of work that are handled by Reserve Bank of India and the Government of India are given in Appendix II.

First Notes - King George VI Series

The first Reserve Bank of India notes were issued, more than two and a half years after it came into existence. There was a reason for this delay. Under Section 22 of the Reserve Bank of India Act, 1934, the Bank had the power to issue Government of India notes till its own notes were ready for issue. On January 20, 1936, the British emperor King George V (whose portrait appeared on Indian currency notes) passed away and was succeeded by King Edward VIII. Notes bearing the portrait of the new King were scheduled for release in the summer of 1937. But developments in Great Britain prevented the release and King Edward VIII abdicated his throne on December 10, 1936. His brother was crowned as King George VI on December 11, 1936.

The first notes issued by Reserve Bank of India were issued in January, 1938. These were the Rupees Five and Ten denomination notes bearing the portrait of King George VI. These were followed by notes in the Rupees 100, 1,000 and 10,000 denominations in the same year.

A Rupees Five note, with picture of King George VI, signed by James B. Taylor, issued by the Reserve Bank of India[50]

These notes bore the words "I PROMISE TO PAY THE BEARER THE SUM OF XXX RUPEES ON DEMAND AT ANY OFFICE OF ISSUE" on the face of the note. The words "GUARANTEED BY THE CENTRAL GOVERNMENT" also appeared at the top beneath the name of Reserve Bank of India. The Governor's signature at the bottom of the note appeared between the words 'FOR THE RESERVE BANK OF INDIA' and 'GOVERNOR'. The notes carried the value of the denomination on the reverse in words in eight different languages in this order: Urdu, Hindi, Bengali, Burmese, Telugu, Tamil, Gujarati and Canarese (Kannada).

However, by that time, Sir Osborne A. Smith had resigned and Sir James Taylor, who was Deputy Governor, had taken over as Governor in July, 1937 for a five-year term.

Interestingly, the first notes issued by Reserve Bank of India bore the signatures of its second Governor, Sir James Taylor. The first Governor, Sir Osborne A. Smith did not sign any bank notes.

During the Second World War, in order to economise the use of note paper, the Reserve Bank of India considered issuing of notes of Rs 20 and Rs 2 and-a-half. Finally, however, notes in the Rupees Two denomination were issued in February, 1943.[51]

In 1942, in the midst of the War, the term of the Governor, Sir James Taylor was extended by five years. But unfortunately, he passed away in 1943 at the young age of 52 years. Forty-seven year old Sir C.D. Deshmukh, a career bureaucrat in the British government, was appointed as the first Indian Governor of the Bank.

During the War, Japanese operations to destabilise Indian currency involved high quality forgeries in the Rupees Ten denomination notes, bearing signatures of Sir C.D. Deshmukh. As a result, new Rupees Ten denomination notes were issued in 1944 with a change in watermark and a full frontal portrait of the King as against a profile portrait earlier.[52]

A Rupees Five note with frontal picture of King George VI, bearing signature of C.D. Deshmukh[53]

By this time, the promissory clause had been changed to "I PROMISE TO PAY THE BEARER ON DEMAND THE SUM OF XXX RUPEES AT ANY OFFICE OF ISSUE".

The last major event in this story before India won its independence was that higher denomination notes of Rupees 500, 1,000 and 10,000 were demonetised in 1946 to curb unaccounted money (more on this in a later chapter).

Bank Notes for Pakistan and Burma (Myanmar)

On August 15, 1947, India became independent with Jawaharlal Nehru as its first Prime Minister. A new country, Pakistan came into existence.

Under the Pakistan (Monetary System and Reserve Bank) Order, 1947 (issued on August 14, 1947), Reserve Bank of India had the sole right to issue notes in Pakistan up to the end of September, 1948. The India notes were to continue to remain legal tender in Pakistan up to that date. The Order provided for the issue by the Bank, from April, 1948, of notes in Pakistan, carrying the inscription 'Government of Pakistan' in English and Urdu.[54]

The arrangement, however, was terminated in June, 1948 due to certain differences between the two countries. Consequently, Reserve Bank of India issued bank notes in the denomination of Rupees 2, 5, 10 and 100 inscribed 'Government of Pakistan' during April to June, 1948. These notes were legal tender in Pakistan only. The central bank for Pakistan, called State Bank of Pakistan, came into being on July 1, 1948.

Although Burma (Myanmar), had separated from India in 1937, the Reserve Bank of India continued to be responsible for its note issue in terms of the India and Burma (Burma Monetary Arrangements) Order, 1937. Initially, Reserve Bank of India issued notes with the overprint 'Legal Tender in Burma Only' but the following year, separate notes were issued for Burma, which were legal tender only in that country.[55] These notes bore signatures of Governor James Taylor and were payable at 'Any Office of Issue in Burma'.

During the World War, between 1942 and 1945, Japanese troops occupied Burma leading to suspension of operations of Reserve Bank of India. The arrangements were restored in 1945 and notes with overprint 'Military Administration of Burma' were issued. On April 1, 1947, the Burma Currency Board became functional. Initially, it was allowed to issue Reserve Bank of India notes with the overprint 'Burmese Currency Board' and 'Legal Tender in Burma Only'. After Burma issued its own currency, these notes were gradually withdrawn and ceased to be legal tender in December, 1952.[56]

First Notes of Independent India: Lion Capitol Replaces King's Portrait

During 1947 to 1949, amidst the turmoil in the aftermath of partition, Reserve Bank of India continued to issue the extant notes. On January 30, 1948 the leader of India's freedom movement, Mahatma Gandhi, was killed in New Delhi as he was emerging after a prayer meeting. It was the time when new symbols had to be chosen for notes for independent India.

At the outset, it was felt that the portrait of the King be replaced with that of Mahatma Gandhi. Designs were prepared to that effect. But the final consensus was for the Lion Capitol of the Asoka Pillar at Sarnath, which replaced the King's portrait.[57] The Lion Capitol (which is also India's national emblem) has continued to be on all currency notes till date, though not as prominently as before.

The issue of the first bank notes of independent India coincided with India becoming a Republic in 1950, with issue of notes in denominations of Rupees 2, 5, 10 and 100. (As mentioned later in the chapter, the first note to be issued in independent India was the One Rupee currency note, issued in 1949). Meanwhile, as Burma had ceased to be part of India, in the language panel on the reverse of the notes mentioning the value of the note, Burmese was replaced by Oriya.

During this period, the Reserve Bank of India was nationalised and became a state-owned institution from January 1, 1949.

Since 1953, the value of the note in Hindi was displayed prominently on the face of the notes.[58] The value of the note in the language panel on the reverse of the note was given in seven languages, in alphabetical order. Urdu, which was appearing at the first place in this list, was now shifted to the last place.

A Rupees Ten note with Lion Capitol in place of the King's picture and value of the note in Hindi on the face, bearing signature of B. Rama Rau

Interestingly, the value of the note, in figures, in Hindi was mentioned as 'Rupiah' (for example, दस रुपया) in the initial note issues of independent India. However, it was argued that the plural should have been 'Rupaiye' (रुपये) instead. The debate regarding the Hindi plural of रुपया was settled in favour of रुपये. Future issues carried the plural रुपये in Hindi,[59] which has continued ever since.

Notes in the higher denominations of Rupees 1,000, 5,000, and 10,000 were reintroduced in 1954. All of these had the Lion Capitol depicted prominently on the face of the note. While the Rupees 1,000 note carried the motif of the Tanjore Temple on the reverse, the Rupees 5,000 note had the motif of Gateway of India and the Rupees 10,000 note had an ornamental design.

Following the States Reorganisation Act, 1956, Indian states were reorganised on linguistic basis. As far as our story is concerned, it led to inclusion of more languages on the currency notes. In December, 1960, the numerical value of the note mentioned in the language panel, was appearing in 13 languages. New languages added were: Assamese, Kashmiri, Malayalam, Marathi, Punjabi and Sanskrit.

Significant Changes in the Sixties

The 1960s were difficult years for the country. With two wars with the neighbours in the first half of the decade (in 1962 and 1965) and back-to-back droughts in 1963-64, the economy was under strain. During the space of 20 months, the nation lost two Prime Ministers, Jawaharlal Nehru in May, 1964 and Lal Bahadur Shastri in January, 1966. Foreign exchange reserves stood at just Rs 78 crores in February 1965 and gold had to be transferred to Reserve Bank of India's Issue Department to shore up foreign assets.[60] In such a backdrop, our story of currency notes merits the narration of four major developments.

First, the sizes of notes were reduced in 1967 due to considerations of economy as the paper on which these were printed was being imported using precious foreign exchange. The reduction in size yielded an annual saving in paper costs of almost 17 per cent.[61]

Second, the text appearing on the notes was shortened. It was necessitated by the cluttered appearance on the smaller notes as well as certain matter felt to have become superfluous over time. Two changes were made in the text appearing on the notes. One, the promissory clause was shortened by excluding the words 'ON DEMAND' and 'AT ANY OFFICE OF ISSUE' therein. The revised promissory clause read 'I PROMISE TO PAY THE BEARER THE SUM OF RUPEES XXX'. Two, the words 'FOR THE RESERVE BANK OF INDIA' were removed from above the Governor's signature. Only the word 'GOVERNOR' remained below the signature. There was also a proposal to remove the words 'GUARANTEED BY THE CENTRAL GOVERNMENT' from the face of the notes. But, it was not implemented for fear of adverse public reaction.[62]

The third development related to the signature of the Governor. So far, the signature of Governor had been appearing in English on the face of all bank notes issued by Reserve Bank of India. It was during the term of Governor L.K. Jha (1967-70) that the Governor's signature started appearing in both English and Hindi on the face of bank notes.

A Rupees Ten note in smaller size with shorter promissory clause, 13 languages in language panel and bi-lingual signature of R.N. Malhotra

The year 1969 brought a major change in the banking scenario of the country with the Prime Minister Indira Gandhi announcing the nationalisation of 14 major banks. It was also the year of Mahatma Gandhi's birth centenary. The fourth and last major development in our story was that Mahatma Gandhi's picture first appeared on bank notes. In 1969, Reserve Bank of India came out with commemorative notes showing Mahatma Gandhi seated cross-legged in the backdrop of the Sevagram Ashram. It was a full picture of Mahatma Gandhi, appearing on the reverse side of the notes, unlike the smiling face that appeared on the obverse of notes issued much later.

New Notes and Motifs in the Seventies

The 1970s saw the introduction of two new denominations of notes to contain the cost of production of notes in circulation. The Rupees 20 denomination was introduced in 1972 and Rupees 50 denomination in 1975.[63] Both carried the picture of Parliament House on the reverse. However, in 1975, a new Rupees 20 note was brought out with the picture of Konark Wheel on the reverse. The new notes were expected to ease the pressure on the Rupees 10 notes.

This decade also saw new motifs on some other denomination notes. The Rupees 10 note introduced in 1975 had flora and fauna motifs on the reverse while the Rupees 5 note carried the picture of a tractor ploughing the field, celebrating the Green Revolution. The Rupees 2 note issued in 1976 showed a picture of satellite Aryabhata, symbolising the country's progress in the field of science and technology.

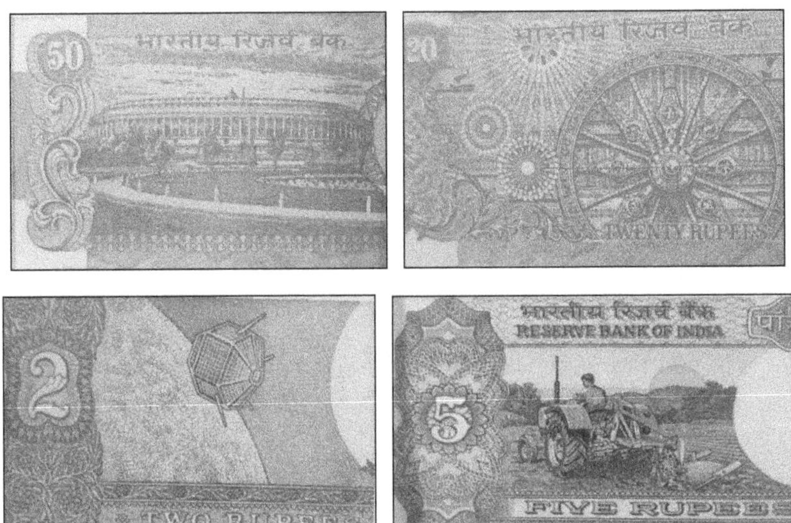

New motifs on notes: Parliament House (on Rs. 50), Konark Wheel (on Rs. 20), Aryabhata satellite (on Rs. 2) and Tractor ploughing a field (on Rs. 5)

In 1977, the Congress party lost the general elections for the first time since independence. The newly-formed Janata Party came to power with Morarji Desai as the Prime Minister. The following year (1978), notes in higher denominations of Rupees 1000, 5,000 and 10,000 were demonetised to weed out black money. This was the second demonetisation in the history of the country (more on this in a later chapter).

The year 1980 saw another small but significant change in the design of currency notes. The legend 'Satyameva Jayate' in Hindi (meaning Truth Alone Shall Prevail) was incorporated under the Lion Capitol (in Hindi) and has continued ever since.

Rupees Five Hundred Note Launched

In October, 1987 bank notes in the Rupees 500 denomination were issued, to contain the volume of Rupees 100 notes in circulation.[64] It was on these notes that Mahatma Gandhi's smiling face first appeared on the obverse of the note prominently on the right side, replacing the Lion Capitol. The Lion Capitol was made smaller and shifted towards the left half of the note.

The first Rs 500 notes with picture of Mahatma Gandhi, bearing signature of R.N.Malhotra

Still More Languages Added on Notes

In 1996, two more languages, Konkani and Nepali, were added to the hitherto 13 languages in which the value of the note was being mentioned in the language panel.[65] This brought the total to fifteen, which has continued unchanged till now.

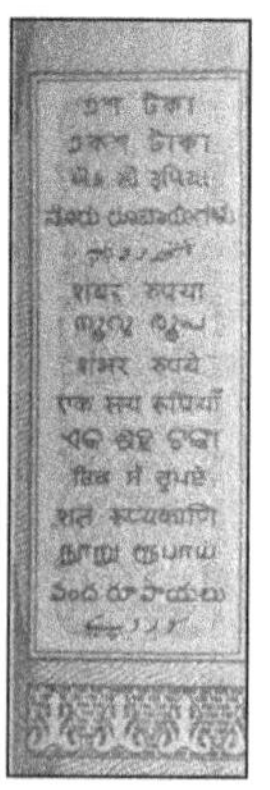

Language panel, with 15 languages, on a Hundred Rupee note

There have been demands to add more languages, especially as more languages have been recognised as official languages under the Eighth Schedule of the Indian Constitution.

Interestingly, the language panel on an Indian currency note gives the value of the note in fifteen different Indian languages in alphabetical order. These are: Assamese, Bengali, Gujarati, Kannada, Kashmiri, Konkani, Malayalam, Marathi, Nepali, Oriya, Punjabi, Sanskrit, Tamil, Telugu and Urdu. In addition, the value is prominently mentioned in Hindi and English. Thus, the value of the note is given in seventeen languages in all.

Mahatma Gandhi Series of Notes Issued

Between 1996 and 2001, different denominations of bank notes in the Mahatma Gandhi Series were issued in a phased manner: Rupees 10 and 100 in June, 1996; Rupees 50 in March and Rupees 500 in October, 1997; Rupees 1,000 in October, 2000; Rupees 20 in August and Rupees 5 in November, 2001. The Rupees 500 note was issued with a changed colour scheme again in November, 2000.

All these notes carried the same picture of the smiling face of Mahatma Gandhi on the face of the note that had appeared first on the 1987 Rupees 500 note. However, in notes of this Series, the Lion Capitol was further reduced in size and shifted to the extreme left corner of the note at the bottom.

A Rupees One Thousand (specimen) note in Mahatma Gandhi Series with Lion Capitol on bottom left, bearing signature of Bimal Jalan

Different motifs were used in notes of different denominations. While the Rupees 1,000 note depicted a collage of India's achievements in science and technology, the Rupees 500 note showed Mahatma Gandhi leading a group of people. The Rupees 100 note had a Himalayan motif (Kanchenjunga peak), Rupees 50 note had the Parliament House and Rupees 20 note had motifs from nature on the reverse. The Rupees 10 note carried fauna motifs showing faces of the elephant, tiger and rhinoceros. There was no change in the motif appearing on Rupees 5 notes.

Interestingly, people have been curious to know the source from where the picture of Mahatma Gandhi that appears on bank notes has been taken. Earlier, it was thought that that it was a drawn caricature. But now, it has been reported that the image was taken and cropped from an actual photograph. The picture was taken in 1946 by an unknown photographer at the Viceroy House (now Rashtrapati Bhawan) and shows Mahatma Gandhi standing next to Lord Fredrick William Pethic-Lawrence. The mirror image of the original picture was used on the Mahatma Gandhi Series bank notes.[66]

Picture of Mahatma Gandhi from which the image for notes has been taken

The watermark in the Mahatma Gandhi Series notes was also changed. The hitherto appearing watermark of the Lion Capitol of the Ashoka Pillar was changed to depict the portrait of Mahatma Gandhi.

In 2005, the Mahatma Gandhi Series notes witnessed enhanced security features, beginning with Rs 100 denomination notes. These included wide colour-shifting machine readable magnetic windowed security thread, see-through register, anti-photocopying feature and more prominent intaglio (raised) printing.[67] Gradually, these were also extended to other denomination notes. Further, since 2005, the year of printing of the notes began to be given on the reverse of the notes.

The Rupee Gets a Distinct Identity

Till 2010, the symbol Rs was being used for the Rupee but it was felt that the Rupee should also have its own distinct symbol like the dollar and the pound. In 2010, ₹ was announced as the new symbol for the Indian Rupee.

New symbol for the Indian Rupee

The symbol is a blend of Devanagri alphabet 'र' (Ra) and Roman alphabet 'R'. The letters are derived from the word 'Rupiah' in Hindi and Rupees in the English language. The horizontal line on top is a unique feature of the Devanagri script. The two horizontal lines taken together, with the white space in between, create a background of the tricolour, the Indian national flag.

Interestingly, the symbol for the Indian Rupee was selected on the basis of a contest held in 2009. The winning entry was chosen out of the over 3,300 entries received. The symbol was created by 32-year old D. Udaya Kumar, who was then a Ph.D student at the Industrial Design Centre, IIT (Indian Institute of Technology), Bombay.

In 2011, the new Rupee symbol was incorporated in the design of Indian bank notes.[68]

A Rupees Twenty note, both sides, in Mahatma Gandhi Series with ₹ symbol, bearing signature of D. Subbarao

Mahatma Gandhi (New) Series

In November, 2016, bank notes in the ₹500 and ₹1,000 denominations were demonetised, that is, their legal status was withdrawn. Consequently, a very large quantity of new currency notes was required to be infused into the system.

Following this, new notes were introduced, which are referred to as the Mahatma Gandhi (New) Series. These notes were slightly smaller than the earlier notes in the Mahatma Gandhi Series. A new denomination, ₹2,000 was introduced and new notes in the ₹500 denomination were issued immediately thereafter. The following year, in August, 2017, another new denomination of ₹200 was introduced. Gradually, new notes in the Mahatma Gandhi (New) Series were also issued in the other denominations, beginning with ₹50 notes in 2017, ₹10 and ₹100 notes in 2018 and ₹20 notes in 2019. No notes in ₹5 denomination were issued in this Series.

Notes in the Mahatma Gandhi (New) Series were issued in new and distinct colours as compared to the earlier notes. While the ₹2,000 note was in magenta, ₹500 was in stone grey, ₹200 in bright yellow, ₹100 in lavender, ₹50 in fluorescent blue, ₹20 in greenish yellow and ₹10 in chocolate brown. No notes have been issued in ₹1,000 denomination since demonetisation and the denomination stands discontinued as of now.

The design of the new notes was somewhat similar to the preceding series of bank notes. The obverse of the notes prominently displayed the picture of Mahatma Gandhi as in the earlier notes. However, the picture was shifted to the centre of the note and was a mirror image of the earlier picture (looking towards the right as against left in the earlier Series). There were other changes too. The Asoka Pillar, which was appearing on the left side on obverse of the notes, was shifted to the right side. The logo of Swachh Bharat Abhiyan (spectacle) appeared on the back of the bank notes of this series. For the first time, the value of the note in numerical form was mentioned in Devnagari (Hindi) script also in addition to the English (Roman) numerals on both sides of the notes.

A Rupees Five Hundred note in Mahatma Gandhi (New) Series, bearing signature of Urjit Patel

The motifs on the reverse of the notes in all denominations except that of ₹2,000 notes depicted prominent historical places denoting the cultural heritage of the country from different states. These were the Sun Temple, Konark, Odisha on ₹10 notes; Ellora Caves, Maharashtra on ₹20 notes; Hampi, Karnataka on ₹50 notes; Rani Ki Vav, Patan, Gujarat on ₹100 notes; Sanchi Stupa, Madhya Pradesh on ₹200 notes; and the Red Fort, New Delhi on ₹500 notes. The ₹2,000 notes carried the motif of Mangalyaan, India's first interplanetary space mission.

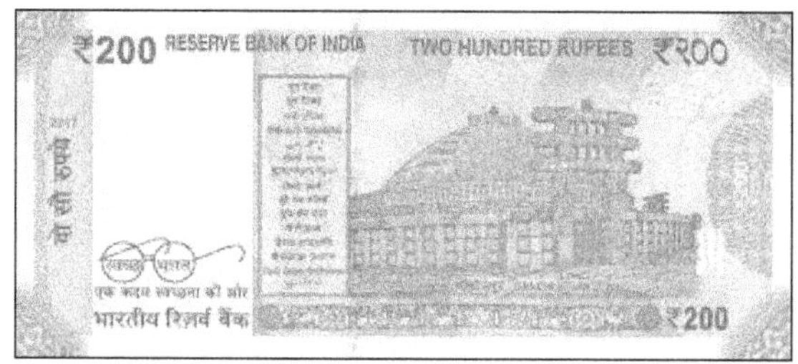

Reverse of Rupees Two Hundred note in Mahatma Gandhi (New) Series, with motif of Sanchi Stupa; Swachha Bharat logo is on the left

The full technical details of the Mahatma Gandhi (New) Series of notes are given in Appendix III.

One Rupee Notes

The One Rupee notes have their own story as these are issued by Government of India and put into circulation by Reserve Bank of India. These notes do not have the promissory clause that appears on other notes and bear the signature of the Finance Secretary, Government of India.

In August 1940, the One Rupee notes (which had been discontinued in 1926) were reintroduced, once again as a war-time measure as a Government note with the status of a rupee coin. The first issues of the note carried the portrait of King George V (who had died in 1936) on the image of a rupee coin of 1935 and bore the signature of Controller of The Currency.

Interestingly, the 1935 One Rupee note is the only note which carries the serial number on the reverse.

A One Rupee note with picture of King George V, signed by J.W.Kelly[69]

Further issues carried the portrait of King George VI.

In 1949, One Rupee notes bearing the picture of Lion Capitol in place of the King's portrait were issued. These were signed by K.R.K. Menon, then Secretary, Ministry of Finance. The colour scheme of the note was changed to violet in 1951.[70] The reverse side of the note carried the picture of the one rupee coin and the language panel.

A One Rupee note of independent India with Lion Capitol, bearing signature of K.R.K. Menon

In 1981, the motif of Sagar Samrat, India's oil exploration rig, as the symbol of industrialisation and progress was depicted on the reverse of the note,[71] in addition to the language panel and the picture of the one rupee coin.

Reverse of One Rupee note with Sagar Samrat motif

The One Rupee notes were discontinued in 1994 but again issued after a 21-year gap in 2015. Predominantly pink green in colour, these notes depicted a replica of One Rupee coin with ₹ symbol on obverse. The motif of Sagar Samrat, which was present on the earlier notes, remained unchanged on the reverse, except for the colour change. The watermark consisted of the Ashoka Pillar, hidden numeral '1' and word 'Bharat'.

A One Rupee note issued again in 2015, after a gap of 21 years, bearing signature of Ratan P. Watal

In 2020, new ₹1 notes were issued in which the replica of One Rupee coin was of 2020 with ₹ symbol.

Endnote

The various changes that have taken place in the design, features and denominations of the notes have reflected the needs of the changing times. As India moves ahead after completing 75 years of independence, it is only a matter of time before more changes take place in our notes.

In the next part of our story, we will look at the infrastructure that has been created over the years for producing notes as per the requirements of the economy. Specifically, we describe the printing presses as well as paper and ink manufacturing units that are required for producing the billions of notes that India requires every year. It will also describe the security features that are embedded in our notes.

Chapter Four

Building Blocks

The process of production of currency begins with Reserve Bank of India estimating the amount of currency required in the economy and conveying it to the printing presses. The notes are then printed in accordance with approved designs. Early currency notes issued in India were printed in England. The first currency note printing press in India was established in 1928 at Nasik (now Nashik in Maharashtra). For several decades, currency production was burdened with problems like inadequate capacity, shortages, and expensive import of paper. The country has come a long way since then and now has an impressive infrastructure for production of currency, led by SPMCIL (Security Printing and Minting Corporation of India Limited) and BRBNML (Bharatiya Reserve Bank Note Mudran Private Limited). This chapter deals with the story of how this infrastructure was created and the important security features built in our notes.

Producing paper currency is like any other manufacturing process, involving planning, infrastructure, raw materials, manufacturing machines, finishing and packing. However, given the sensitive nature of the final product, the process is generally not publicised enough and very scanty details are made available in public domain. This part of the story is, therefore, constructed on the basis of available information, which can be shared with all.

How Many Notes to Print

The decision on how many notes are to be printed during a year is taken on an annual basis. Every year, in consultation with Government of India, the Reserve Bank of India decides the quantity of notes that is required to be printed during the following year. The demand for currency is largely driven by economic activity as reflected in the real Gross Domestic Product (GDP) growth besides inflation, interest rate, growth of digital payments, etc.

Estimation of demand for currency has a bearing on various macroeconomic activities. Short term estimates (less than 1 year) are useful to track the seasonal variation and unexpected but transitory changes in the requirement of currency. Medium term estimates (1-2 years) are useful for planning annual requirement of fresh currency. Long term demand (5-10 years) is required for capacity planning of the note presses and has to take into account the possibility of changes in the denomination structure.[72]

The total demand for currency is the sum total of its two components, namely, incremental demand (or transactional demand) and replacement demand. Estimation of incremental demand is done by combining different econometric models assuming exogenous variables, such as real GDP growth, inflation rate, call rate, and digital/alternate payment growth. The replacement demand is projected based on the denomination-wise estimated lifespan of banknotes. Finally, the total demand projection is arrived at by adjusting for contingency demand (in case of emergency) keeping view of the existing stock of currency with the Reserve Bank of India.[73] The withdrawal plan of certain series of notes is also factored in the indent, whenever required. The value of projected banknotes is then apportioned to different denominations based on the trends of their past issues.

The requirement of notes is then communicated to the printing presses (through the Government of India) as indents for supply of notes. However, the printing presses may not be able to supply to supply the entire quantity required due to their own constraints.

As specified in Section 25 of the Reserve Bank of India Act, 1934, the design, form and material of bank notes are decided by the Government of India based on the recommendations of the Central Board of the Reserve Bank of India. Special care is taken in the choice of the size, colour and design of the notes to enable the public to distinguish the notes of different denominations easily at a glance.[74]

Currency Note Press, Nashik

Early currency notes used in India were got printed in England from either Thomas de la Rue, an English firm or the Bank of England. The story of printing currency notes for India within the country began in 1922, when the Master of Bombay Mint and the Controller of Printing and Stationery, Government of India, Delhi, were appointed to explore the feasibility of printing notes in India. Based on their report in 1924, the Government of India arranged to set up an experimental press.[75]

In 1925, the India Security Press was established at Nasik Road in Maharashtra for producing all security documents required by Posts and Telegraphs, Law Courts, etc. Nasik Road was selected as the site for the Press as it was situated on the main railway line having direct access to all parts of India and there were no sudden and large changes in humidity and temperature. The Press was located close to the railway station.

The Currency Note Press of the India Security Press was commissioned for printing currency notes in April, 1928. The first notes printed there were in the Rupees Five denomination and issued from Kanpur Circle in October, 1928. This was followed by notes in the Rupees 100 denomination.[76]

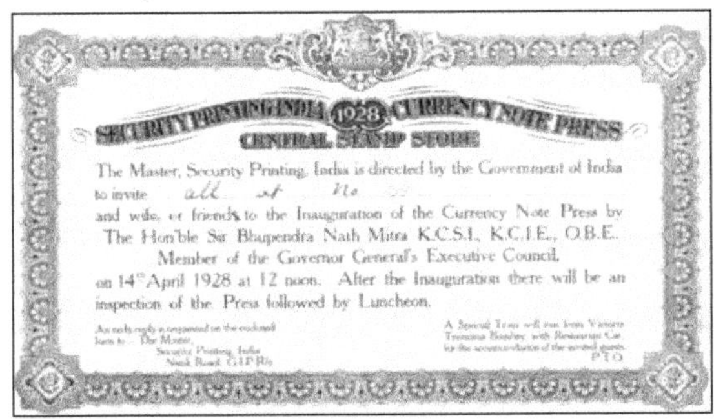

SECURITY PRINTING INDIA 1928 CURRENCY NOTE PRESS
CENTRAL STAMP STORE

The Master, Security Printing, India is directed by the Government of India to invite *all at No* ... and wife, or friends to the Inauguration of the Currency Note Press by The Hon'ble Sir Bhupendra Nath Mitra K.C.S.I., K.C.I.E., O.B.E. Member of the Governor General's Executive Council. on 14th April 1928 at 12 noon. After the Inauguration there will be an inspection of the Press followed by Luncheon.

An early reply is requested on the enclosed form to – The Master, Security Printing, India Nasik Road G.I.P.Rly

A Special Train will run from Victoria Terminus Bombay with Restaurant Car for the accommodation of the invited guests. P.T.O.

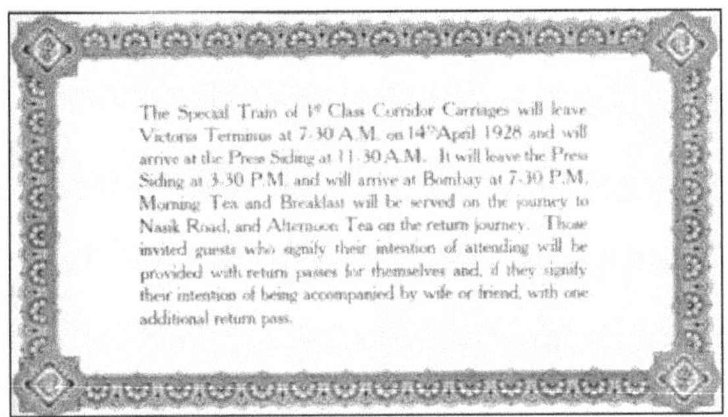

The Special Train of 1st Class Corridor Carriages will leave Victoria Terminus at 7-30 A.M. on 14th April 1928 and will arrive at the Press Siding at 11-30 A.M. It will leave the Press Siding at 3-30 P.M. and will arrive at Bombay at 7-30 P.M. Morning Tea and Breakfast will be served on the journey to Nasik Road, and Afternoon Tea on the return journey. Those invited guests who signify their intention of attending will be provided with return passes for themselves and, if they signify their intention of being accompanied by wife or friend, with one additional return pass.

Photograph of both sides of the official invitation to the inauguration of the Currency Note Press, Nasik Road on April 14, 1928[77]

By 1931-32, notes of all denominations were being printed there. For the first few years, the Press was printing currency notes issued by the then Government of India. Among its milestones, the Currency Note Press mentions printing of the first notes for Reserve Bank of India in 1938, bearing the signature of Governor, Sir James Taylor.[78]

Interestingly, for the inauguration of the Currency Note Press, a Special Train was run on April 14, 1928 for the invited guests, leaving Victoria Terminus (VT) Station, Bombay (now Mumbai) at 7.30 in the morning to reach Nasik Road at 11.30 am. On return, the train left Nasik at 3.30 in the afternoon to reach back at 7.30 pm. Morning tea and breakfast was served during the outward journey and afternoon tea on the return journey. The train had 1st Class Corridor Carriages with Restaurant Car.[79]

In order to meet the growing demand for currency notes arising from the growth of the economy, the existing Press was further expanded and shifted to a new location in 1962.

Currency Note Press, Nashik (Maharashtra)

Bank Note Press, Dewas

In 1974, nearly five decades after the first Press was set up, another currency printing press was built to meet the increasing requirements of currency notes. It was located at Dewas in Madhya Pradesh and had an annual capacity of printing 2,495 million pieces of bank notes. Named as the Bank Note Press, its design, machinery and technology were obtained from M/s De La Rue Giori and Koeing & Bauer (now known as KBA Giori S.A. Switzerland). The Press was designed to produce world class, high quality bank notes to impede forgery. For this, it incorporated higher security features and latest modern techniques like intaglio printing and dry offset printing with security features such as continuous bleed of tints, interlock designs, see-through designs and use of fluorescent inks.[80]

Bank Note Press, Dewas (Madhya Pradesh)

The first consignment of notes from this Press was remitted to the Reserve Bank of India in March, 1975. Initially, the Press was printing Rs 20, 50, 100 and 500 denomination notes with intaglio designs.

Against the backdrop of a phenomenal growth in currency circulation in the 1980s, there was a steep rise in demand for fresh currency/ bank notes in the early 1990s. Supply constraints were acute in the case of higher denomination notes. The production capacities of the two note-printing presses at Nasik and Dewas had, however, remained static, and hence these presses were unable to meet the indent for fresh notes.[81] The quality of notes in circulation in the market was deteriorating with torn and repaired notes being used in transactions.

Two New Presses at Mysore and Salboni

As a result, the Government decided to establish two new bank note printing presses, one at Mysore in Karnataka and the second at Salboni in West Bengal. The New Note Press Project, which was initiated by Government of India, was transferred to Reserve Bank of India in 1989. In 1995, the Reserve Bank of India formed a wholly owned subsidiary called Bharatiya Reserve Bank Note Mudran Private Limited (BRBNMPL) for setting up and running the two new presses. Both the presses became fully operational during 1999-2000. However, before that, there was a severe supply crunch of currency notes.

The Dewas and Nasik presses had to be modernised. The supply of fresh notes from them declined: during 1995 to 1997, they could meet only around one-fourth of the value of indented requirement of currency. In order to bridge the demand-supply gap for fresh notes it was decided to import 2,000 million pieces of Rs 100 and 1,600 million pieces of Rs 500 notes from abroad.[82]

Interestingly, during 1997-98, 2,000 million pieces of Rs 100 and 1600 million pieces of Rs 500 were printed in other countries to meet the increased demand and to act as buffer. The details were:

Rs 100: (i) American Banknote Company (USA): 635 million pieces, (ii) Thomas De La Rue, UK: 1365 million pieces;

Rs 500: Giesecke & Devrient Consortium (Germany): 1600 million pieces.[83]

The Parliamentary Committee on Public Undertakings, in its Sixth Report on Security Printing and Minting Corporation of India Limited (SPMCIL) 2009-10, called it an unprecedented, unconventional and uncalled for measure and expressed its strong resentment, while recommending that outsourcing printing of currency notes should never be resorted to in future.[84]

After commencement of operations at presses at Mysore and Salboni and modernisation of the presses at Nashik (earlier Nasik) and Dewas the combined capacity of the four presses was augmented considerably so as to meet future requirements, besides current demand, with the flexibility to achieve an appropriate denomination mix. The combined installed capacity of these note presses was about 18,000 million pieces per annum.[85]

In 2005, the Union Cabinet approved the decision to corporatize the two printing presses at Nashik and Dewas, besides two security presses, one security paper mill and four mints. Accordingly, the Security Printing and Minting Corporation of India Limited

(SPMCIL) was set-up in January, 2006 with its registered office in New Delhi.

At present, in 2024, the printing of currency notes in the country is done through four printing presses: one each at Nashik and Dewas under the SPMCIL and one each at Salboni and Mysuru under BRBNMPL. During 2023-24, these four printing presses supplied a total of 243,000 lakh (24.30 billion) pieces of banknotes to the Reserve Bank of India. Over one-third of these notes (9.0 billion pieces) were of ₹500 denomination.[86]

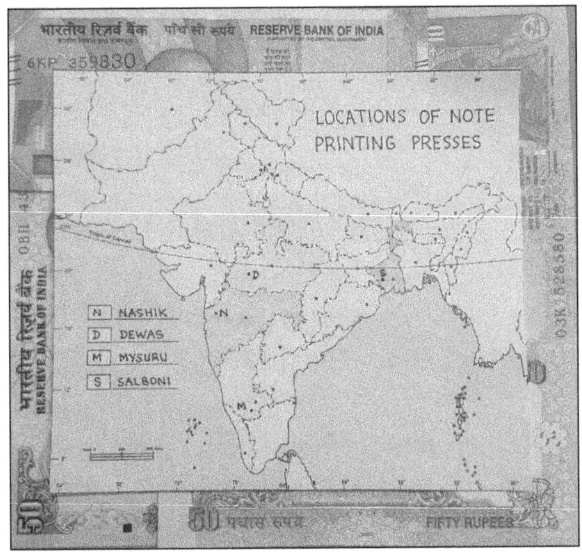

Map showing locations of note printing presses: Nashik in Maharashtra, Dewas in Madhya Pradesh, Mysuru in Karnataka and Salboni in West Bengal

Security Paper Mill, Hoshangabad

Even though India was printing its own currency, the paper used for the purpose was being imported, costing the nation valuable foreign exchange. The question of manufacturing currency note paper in India was pursued by Reserve Bank of India and Government during the Second World War. But difficulties of locating a suitable place with perennial freshwater supply in the vicinity of the Nasik Printing Press and of procuring and shipping the necessary machinery under wartime conditions halted further progress.[87]

In May, 1950, Portals, a British firm which for over 100 years had supplied note paper to India, offered to set up a small pilot security paper plant if the government met its cost. However, it was only in 1962 when a contract was awarded to Portals to erect a mill in Hoshangabad.[88] The decision for selecting this site in Madhya Pradesh was taken considering its compliance with prerequisites like land, water, electricity, transportation and manpower. The Security Paper Mill at Hoshangabad in Madhya Pradesh was commissioned in June, 1967 for manufacturing high quality paper for bank notes and non-judicial stamp papers.

Even over forty years later, the quantity of paper being produced by the Mill was hardly sufficient for the country's requirements although the country had sufficient capacity for producing its currency notes. In 2008-09, Reserve Bank of India had got 15 billion notes printed through the four printing presses.[89] However, the paper being used for printing the currency notes was largely being imported, costing precious foreign exchange. Till as late as 2010, the country was producing hardly five per cent of the 18,000 metric tonnes of paper required for currency notes from the Hoshangabad Security Paper Mill.[90]

The remaining requirements of paper were being imported. While giving information to the Sixth Parliamentary Committee in 2009, the Chairman, SPMCIL had informed that "since independence,..., there was only one paper supplier, De La Rue of the United Kingdom, to this country till mid 1990s. Presently we are having six paper suppliers."[91] It was revealed to the Parliament during April 2010 that the country was importing paper used for printing currency notes from suppliers in Italy, France, The Netherlands, Germany, Sweden and United Kingdom.[92]

New Bank Note Paper Mill at Mysuru

Around that time, it was decided to set up a state-of-the-art technology paper line with a capacity of 6,000 metric tonnes in the Security Paper Mill, Hoshangabad. It was also decided to set up a new banknote paper mill at Mysuru (earlier Mysore) in Karnataka. The project for the new mill was envisaged as a joint venture between the BRBNMPL and the SPMCIL, the two agencies collectively responsible for printing of all currency notes in the country. The foundation stone for the proposed Mill was laid by the then Finance Minister Pranab Mukherjee in 2010.

The new paper line at Hoshangabad started commercial production in 2015. The new mill at Mysuru, named Bank Note Paper Mill India Private Limited (BNPMIPL), started commercial production in 2016.

The BNPMIPL is engaged in producing paper for bank notes with an installed capacity of 12,000 metric tonnes per annum. The Mill uses state-of-art technology in special purpose machines. In order to make the paper robust and secured, exclusive security features are incorporated. The special watermarks designed and created during manufacturing process are unique and makes the paper highly difficult to reproduce. Special type equipment and unique process is used for incorporation of windowed and embedded security threads.

Bank Note Paper Mill India Private Limited, Mysuru (Karnataka)

In 2019-20, the company had produced 15,874 metric tonnes (132 per cent of rated capacity) of banknote paper, thereby meeting the entire demand of the four printing presses and stopping import of paper.[93]

Polymer Notes

The two paper mills have helped in making the country self-sufficient in its requirements of paper for currency notes. However, over the last couple of decades, some countries have done away with paper notes and introduced polymer notes in order to increase their life span and reduce counterfeiting. Even the Reserve Bank of India had considered introducing polymer notes in India in the ₹10 denomination, but the proposal could not materialise, for reasons which have not been made public so far.

Interestingly, to increase the circulation life of banknotes, particularly in the small denominations, the Reserve Bank of India toyed with the idea of introducing polymer notes in the country for several years. In 2009, it called for an Expression of Interest from global manufacturers for one billion polymer banknotes of ₹10 denomination. A year later, it reported introduction of polymer notes on a 'field trial' basis in select locations, based on differing climatic conditions. In 2013, it was stated that the field trials would be conducted in Kochi, Mysuru, Jaipur, Bhubaneswar and Shimla. In 2014-15, the Request for Proposal for polymer notes in the ₹10 denomination was issued and its technical evaluation undertaken. However, certain technical infirmities emerged and the process could not be taken further. The following year, the project was taken up by the Bharatiya Reserve Bank Note Mudran Private Ltd (BRBNMPL) and the Security Printing and Minting Corporation of India Ltd (SPMCIL).[94] But surprisingly, since then, there has been total silence on the issue, indicating that the proposal has been quietly buried.

In 2018-19, Reserve Bank of India announced introduction of varnished banknotes of ₹100 denomination on a field trial basis in order to increase their lifespan. However, the printing of these notes was delayed due to disruptions on account of the Covid pandemic and certain other developments.[95]

Manufacturing of Inks

Highly specialised inks are used in the printing of currency notes. An Ink Factory Unit was established in the Dewas Press in 1973 to manufacture security inks. The factory, which produces offset, numbering and intaglio inks, was taken up for modernisation and expansion in 2009-10. In 2010-11, the factory produced its highest ever production of 298 metric tonnes of security inks. Even up to 2014-15, India produced Offset and Intaglio inks while Optically Variable Ink was being imported.

In 2018, the BRBNMPL set up an Ink Manufacturing Unit named Varnika at Mysuru with an annual production capacity of 1,500 metric tonnes. Dry offset, intaglio, numbering and colour shifting intaglio inks used in the printing of banknotes are being manufactured at this factory.[96] Since 2019-20, the entire requirement of these inks has been met by this Unit. During 2020, with the installation of in-house varnish making plant, the company became self-sufficient in different type of varnishes required including varnish for colour shifting intaglio inks. This marks a significant step towards backward integration and achieving its ultimate goal of complete indigenisation of banknote production processes.[97]

Cost of Note Printing

While people are interested in knowing how much it costs to print a single note, authentic data in this regard is not easily available. The Reserve Bank of India gives the total expenditure incurred in printing of notes as well as the total number of notes supplied by the various printing presses during the year in its Annual Reports. Derived figures from these sets of data show that the expenditure incurred by the Reserve Bank of India on printing a note was ₹2.24 during 2021-22.[98] A few years back, in 2014-15, the expenditure incurred was ₹1.59.[99]

Some information is also available on the basis of certain replies to queries made under the Right to Information (RTI) Act. In response to a query filed under the RTI Act by a business correspondent of a financial daily, the Currency Note Press had replied that the standard cost of printing one currency note in the denomination of ₹500 was ₹2.65 in 2019-20. Similarly, the cost of printing one note each of ₹10, ₹20, ₹50 and ₹100 denomination was ₹0.94, ₹0.90, ₹1.22 and ₹1.99 respectively.[100]

Interestingly, the one rupee currency note, which was re-introduced in 2015 after a gap of 21 years, costs more than its face value. This was revealed in a RTI (Right to Information) query filed by activist Subhash Chandra Agrawal in 2015. The information was given by the Security Printing and Minting Corporation of India. It said, "The cost of one rupee note is Rs 1.14 (provisionally and unaudited) as determined in accordance with the principle of costing and costing module."[101]

Numbering of Notes

Every note produced has its own number. Each packet of fresh notes printed in the press contains 100 serially numbered notes (except 'Star' series notes, as explained below). The number of a note consists of a mix of alphabets and numerals, consisting of a prefix and a number. In the denominations up to ₹20, the prefix consists of two digits followed by one alphabet, such as 16K or 29B. In denominations from ₹50 and above, the prefix consists of one digit followed by two alphabets, such as 9AB or 1GH. The prefix is followed by a number from 000001 to 1000000 in all notes. In addition the number panel may also have an alphabet in capital letter, which appears in a lighter shade, called the inset letter, such as 'E' or 'S'. The Mahatma Gandhi (New) Series of notes carry the number of the note (after the prefix) in ascending size of numerals, from left to right while all characters in the prefix remain of the same size.

Number panel of (on left) ₹5 Mahatma Gandhi Series note with prefix of two numerals and an alphabet (14A) and all numerals of same size with inset letter 'L' and (on right) ₹2000Mahatma Gandhi (New) Series note with prefix of one numeral and two alphabets(4DD) and numerals in ascending size from left to right with inset letter 'R'.

Interestingly, in the prefix, only twenty alphabets are used. No prefix with alphabet O, I and J are used as these are confused for numerals. Also alphabets X, Y and Z are not used to round the number of prefixes to twenty or multiple of ten for accounting purposes. The same twenty alphabets are also used for insets. The inset denotes the printing press where the note has been printed. For security reasons, the Reserve Bank of India does not reveal which inset letters are assigned to which printing press. But it is assumed that plain (no inset) and the alphabets A, B, C, D are allotted to Mysore, E, F, G, H, K to Dewas, L, M, N, P, Q to Salboni and R, S, T, U, V to Nasik.[102] (However, alphabet W is not mentioned in the above allocation.)

Earlier, in 2006, the Reserve Bank of India had introduced the 'Star' series of notes in denominations of Rs 10, 20 and 50 for replacement of defectively printed notes. These notes had an additional character, namely * (star), in the number panel between the prefix and the serial number, for example, 65B*441993. The purpose was to reduce the cost of printing notes. Fresh note packets containing the 'Star' series notes would have notes not in serial order but (like other fresh note packets) have 100 notes per packet.[103] In 2009, 'Star' series notes were introduced for the Rs 100 denomination too.

*A Star Series note with * mark between prefix and number*

Security Features of Notes

The issuers of currency notes have always endeavoured to make the notes secure so that these cannot be easily replicated. This has been done by using paper with special features, sophisticated inks and advanced printing techniques, besides giving them unique numbers.

Most people use notes without giving much thought to their unique features. However, since the last couple of decades, the Reserve Bank of India has been proactively engaged in educating the public about the various features of currency notes. This awareness is expected to help the common people differentiate between a genuine and a forged note.

Early security features used in currency notes were the watermark, printed signature and registration of notes, which were used in the Victoria Portrait Series of notes. Security thread was introduced as a security feature in notes for the first time in 1944 in the King George VI series of notes.

Until 1956, it was the practice for notes of denominations of Rs 100 and above in circulation to be 'registered' in the books of the Reserve Bank of India, Issue Department. A record of all such notes issued and cancelled was maintained. However, with Rs 100 notes making up nearly 40 per cent of the total circulation of notes by 1954, the work in the 'registration' sections (of Issue Department) had fallen into tremendous arrears. It was felt that more complex design and better quality paper were better safeguards against forgeries and the practice was abandoned in 1956.[104]

New and improved security features were introduced in the Mahatma Gandhi Series of bank notes, beginning 1995. The Ashoka Pillar watermark was replaced by the portrait of Mahatma Gandhi with multi-directional lines. Some of the features were modified in 2005: for example, in the watermark an electrolyte mark showing the denominational numeral was added.

After demonetisation of higher denomination notes in 2016, notes of new design in Mahatma Gandhi (New) Series were introduced. The main security features present on these notes are as follows[105]:

- *Watermark:* This consists of an image that is visible when the bank note is held up against the light, which is created during the manufacturing process such that it is an integral part of the paper. These notes contain the Mahatma Gandhi portrait with the denomination numeral (electrotype) watermark.
- *Security Thread:* The notes of denominations of ₹100 and above have a machine-readable windowed demetalised clear text magnetic security thread. The colour of the thread changes from green to blue when viewed from different angles. In case of ₹100 denomination, the thread has a width of 2 mm while for higher denominations its width is 3 mm. The ₹2000 notes contain a windowed security thread alternately visible on the obverse with

the inscriptions 'Bharat' (in Hindi), '2000' and 'RBI', but totally embedded on the reverse. The ₹500, 200 and 100 notes have a security thread with similar visible features and inscriptions 'Bharat' (in Hindi), and 'RBI'. When held against the light, the security thread on these notes can be seen as one continuous line. The ₹10, 20 and 50 notes contain fully embedded windowed security thread with the inscription 'Bharat' (in Hindi), and 'RBI'. Notes issued prior to the introduction of the Mahatma Gandhi Series have a plain, fully embedded security thread.

- *Latent Image:* The latent image is a security feature that is concealed within the note. It is visible only when it is held horizontally at eye level. In notes of denomination 100 and above, the latent image with the denomination of the numeral is visible at the bottom left hand corner, when the note is held at 45 degree angle from the eye level.
- *Micro lettering:* This feature can be seen only under a magnifying glass. It appears on the left shoulder of the Mahatma Gandhi portrait with inscriptions 'India' and 'भारत'. Micro letters can also be seen on the motifs in the reverse side of the notes.
- *Intaglio Printing:* Raised printing which are due to deposits of ink and can be felt on touch are called intaglio printing. In notes of denominations of 100 and above, the portrait of Mahatma Gandhi, the Ashoka Pillar Emblem, Guarantee clause, Governor's signature, Promise clause, RBI Emblem, bleed lines and the identification marks are in intaglio.
- *Identification Mark:* These are features that appear on the higher denomination notes in intaglio on the right side to help the visually impaired identify the denomination of notes. It is a triangle in notes of ₹100, an 'H' shape in ₹200, a circle in ₹500 and a rectangle in ₹2000.
- *Fluorescence:* This is a special security feature in which optical fibres and florescent ink is used which glows when exposed

to ultraviolet light The number panels of the notes are printed in fluorescent ink and the note also contains optic fibres, both of which glow when the note is held under an ultra violet lamp. The optical fibres are dual coloured (i.e. each fibre shows two colours) and are in combination of red/ yellow and blue/green.

- *Optically Variable Ink:* The rupee symbol and the denomination in the banknotes of denomination ₹200 and above is written in the obverse of the note in colour shifting ink (green to blue).
- *See-through Register:* The see-through register is a design that is printed partially on both sides of the note, exactly opposite of each other, and looks like one single design when seen against the light.
- *Ascending font of numbers:* This is a new feature wherein the font size of the number (excluding prefix) in the number panel is increasing from left to right.
- *Angular Bleed Lines:* This feature is seen in the notes issued since 2016. It is a set of lines in raised prints at the left and right hand edges of the note slightly above the Ashoka Emblem. The number and blocks/sets of these lines vary as per the denomination - 4 lines (in 2 sets of 2) in notes of 100, 4 lines (in sets of 2 separated by two circles) in notes of ₹200, 5 lines (sets of 2-1-2) in ₹500, 7 lines (sets of 1-2-1-2-1) in ₹2000.

The Reserve Bank of India has brought out posters depicting the security features present in notes of various denominations for the general information of the public. These posters are available on https://paisaboltahai.rbi.org.in.

A Reserve Bank of India poster explaining the security features of the ₹500 note

Mobile Aided Note Identifier

Although the Mahatma Gandhi and Mahatma Gandhi (New) Series of notes have specific features to aid the visually impaired, there was a felt need to make the identification easier for such persons. This was sought to be achieved in January 2020, when the Reserve Bank of India launched a mobile app (application) called MANI (Mobile Aided Note Identifier). It has made the currency notes more accessible to the visually impaired for facilitating their day-to-day transactions.

The app is capable of identifying the denominations of Mahatma Gandhi Series and Mahatma Gandhi (New) Series notes by checking front or reverse side or part of the note, including half folded notes, in a broad range of light conditions. The notification can be through audio in Hindi/ English as well as non-sonic mode such as vibration. A useful feature of the app, available for free, is that it does not require internet and can work in offline mode.[106]

The app has been developed by Daffodil Software and uses Artificial Intelligence technology. Within a month of its launch, the app had over 350,000 downloads.[107] In addition to Hindi and English, the app notifies the banknote denomination in 11 regional languages.[108]

Endnote

Over time, technological developments have led to significant changes in the note production processes in the country. Today, India is self-reliant in the manufacture of currency notes to meet the requirements of its 1.38 billion people and its robust and growing economy. In fact, after China, India is the world's largest producer and consumer of currency notes.

Just like us human beings, every single note produced has its own unique life, from its birth (production) to death (destruction). The next part of our story would deal with how, after being produced, the notes undertake their life journey through the economy, passing various stages of their life-cycle, from production to destruction. It is a fascinating journey, and one that has been impacted by technological changes.

Chapter Five

Life Cycle

This part of the story tells of the life cycle of currency notes: their journey from the vaults of the Reserve Bank of India to currency chests, banks, ATMs and into the wallets and hands of the public. During this journey, they become old and soiled and come to the end of their useful life. It is time for them to take the return journey back to the Reserve Bank of India, where they are examined, verified and, lastly, destroyed. The increasing volume of currency in the economy has over the years has necessitated changing methods in currency processing. Technology is increasingly being used in the process of handling of currency notes. There are sophisticated counting, sorting, verifying and shredding machines through which the currency notes have to pass during their life time. Unlike in the past, when currency notes were burnt at the end of their life-span, in the present times, the notes are shredded and converted into briquettes.

Although physically, the currency notes take birth in the various printing presses, at that time they are mere pieces of printed paper and not part of the currency in circulation. In technical terms, these are called 'note forms'. They remain such till they move out into the economy and become part of money in circulation. For this, these notes may have to travel thousands of kilometres through various modes before they can achieve the status of becoming currency in circulation.

The Journey Begins

The outward journey begins when packed crates containing 'note forms' move out of the gates of the printing presses. Their first destination is one of the 19 Issue Offices of the Reserve Bank of India, located at Ahmedabad, Belapur (Navi Mumbai), Bengaluru, Bhopal, Bhubaneswar, Chandigarh, Chennai, Guwahati, Hyderabad, Jaipur, Jammu, Kanpur, Kolkata, Lucknow, Mumbai, Nagpur, New Delhi, Patna and Thiruvanantpuram.

Although the Reserve Bank of India has its offices at several other locations in the country, the Issue Offices (which deal with currency) are limited to the above centres. Notably, while the state of Maharashtra has three Issue Offices, Uttar Pradesh has two while the seven north-eastern states have just a single office amongst them. In the Issue Offices of the Reserve Bank of India, these notes (which are still 'note forms') are securely kept in huge vaults, called Fresh Note Vaults.

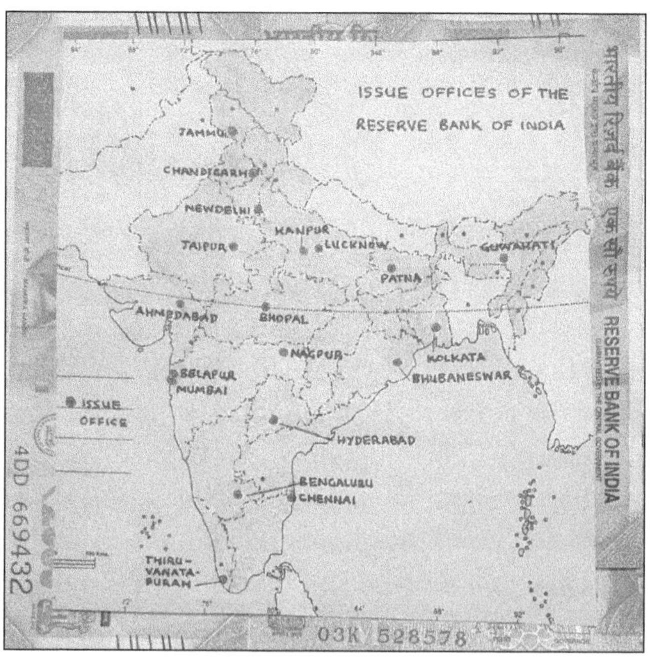

Location of the 19 Issue Offices of the Reserve Bank of India

The magnitude of the journey of currency notes to meet the transaction needs of a nation of 1.38 billion is truly enormous. Take, for example, the currency notes supplied by the printing presses in a year. In 2023-24, the printing presses in the country supplied 2,43,000 lakh (24.30 billion) pieces of currency notes.[109] Such a voluminous quantity of notes is initially transported from the presses to the 19 Issue Offices of Reserve Bank of India. From there, these notes are moved to over 2,700 currency chests, about 140,000 bank branches and 220,000 ATMs spread across the length and breadth of the country and ultimately to members of the public in order to cater to their monetary requirements.

The logistics involved in this mammoth exercise involves high degree of security, precision and secrecy. Every day of the year, hundreds of transactions involving movement of currency notes take place. That no untoward incident takes place is a testimony to the sound systems and procedures adopted in this process.

Currency Chests

The first destination as the notes move out from the vaults of the Reserve Bank of India is a specified bank branch, known as a currency chest. As Reserve Bank of India has its Issue Offices at very limited centres in the country, it has arrangements with banks to store notes on its behalf in their vaults. These branches, which are the extended arms of Reserve Bank of India, are called currency chest branches. The currency chest bank branches have strong and secure vaults with technical specifications as prescribed by the Reserve Bank of India from time to time to store the currency. Within the vaults, the notes are stored in secured currency bins.

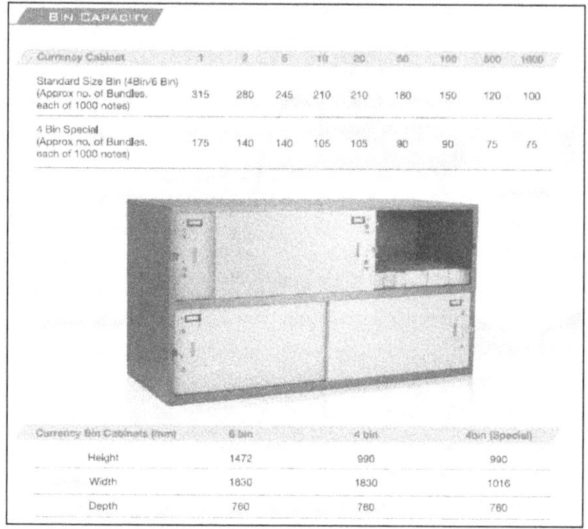

BIN CAPACITY

Currency Cabinet	1	2	5	10	20	50	100	500	1000
Standard Size Bin (4Bin/6 Bin) (Approx no. of Bundles, each of 1000 notes)	315	280	245	210	210	180	150	120	100
4 Bin Special (Approx no. of Bundles, each of 1000 notes)	175	140	140	105	105	90	90	75	75

Currency Bin Cabinets (mm)	6 bin	4 bin	4bin (Special)
Height	1472	990	990
Width	1830	1830	1016
Depth	760	760	760

A common type of currency storage bin used to store notes in currency chests

In 2019, the Reserve Bank of India prescribed minimum standards for setting up new currency chests by banks[110]; these were done to ensure large-sized currency chests with adequate processing capacity and adoption of automation and implementing technological solutions.

Historically, currency chests were with the erstwhile Imperial Bank of India (later State Bank of India) and the Treasuries of the Government. The number of currency chests was about 1,300 at the end of 1939.[111] For a number of decades, currency chests were only with the public sector banks. It was only in 1990-91 when scheduled private sector banks were also allowed to establish currency chests.[112] In 2003-04, foreign banks were also permitted to operate currency chests.[113] But still, even now, the public sector banks have a predominant share of currency chests.

At the end of March 2024, there were 2,794 currency chests in the country. Of them, 2,553 (over 91 per cent) were branches of State Bank of India and other public sector banks. The private sector banks accounted for only 224 currency chests. Co-operative banks, Regional

Rural Banks and foreign banks shared just 16 currency chests amongst themselves. Reserve Bank of India itself had a lone currency chest.[114]

The movement of currency to the currency chest can be by road, rail or air, depending upon the conditions. The remittance, as the consignment of currency is called, is accompanied by adequate police security and a representative of the Reserve Bank of India, who hands over the same to the representative of the currency chest. The representative of the currency chest takes over the remittance after due counting and verification as per procedures. The quantity of currency notes sent to the currency chest depends upon its requirements, which are submitted to the Reserve Bank of India as indents on annual basis.

The Reserve Bank of India has also adopted the Hub and Spoke model for distribution of currency notes to currency chests. Under this model, fresh note remittances are sent to larger currency chests, which meet the currency needs of a designated area, such as a district, identified as hub chests and these, in turn, supply notes to smaller currency chests in their vicinity which act like spokes in the distribution model.[115]

Following the demonetisation of 2016, notes were directly supplied from the presses to more than 100 currency chests to improve availability.[116] This measure was necessitated due to extreme shortage of currency in the economy and resulted in cutting down the time required for the notes to reach the public.

The currency notes held in the currency chest belong to Reserve Bank of India and are accounted for, as such. Only when they are withdrawn from the currency chest, they become part of the balance of the concerned bank and a part of the currency in circulation. From the bank's balance, these notes move out to the customers of the bank when they come to the bank for their cash requirements.

Reserve Bank of India provides licenses to banks for opening currency chests. As these balances form part of the Reserve Bank of

India's balances, these are subjected to periodical inspections by its officers. Currency chests have also to abide by the rules and regulations prescribed by Reserve Bank of India for their operation and security. These include police patrolling, CCTV cameras, alarm systems and proper upkeep of the currency notes in secure, locked bins in double custody of two officials of the bank. The balances are required to be verified at periodical intervals by independent officials, not connected with the currency chest and auditors.

The notes lie in the currency chests till there is a demand for their withdrawal. They may be withdrawn by the currency chest branch for its own requirements or for the requirements of another branch, to which these are sent as required.

Bank Branches

Only a limited number of bank branches have currency chests. All the remaining bank branches are linked to one of these specific currency chests for their requirement of notes. Thus, each currency chest may have dozens of bank branches which are linked to it and to which the currency chest has to supply currency notes as per the requirement of the branch.

The outward journey of currency notes thus continues further from the currency chests to different bank branches. There these notes lie as part of the cash balance of the bank till a customer comes to take them as part of her requirement of cash. It is at this stage that these notes come into contact with the public, where these get a temporary 'residence' in the wallets or pockets of the people.

Automated Teller Machines (ATMs)

Some currency notes move from the bank branch to one of the numerous ATMs attached to the branch for their requirement of currency notes. Such notes are transported from the bank branch to the ATM in secure vans and accompanied by security personnel and filled in the various cassettes of the ATM. There these notes remain till a customer visits the ATM to withdraw cash. Thus, from the ATM, these currency notes come to the hands of the public for being used by them for their monetary transactions.

At the end of March 2022, there were 2,15,061 ATMs in the country[117], much more than the number of bank branches. So, this is the most commonly used mode by people for obtaining their requirement of currency. In addition to providing cash withdrawals, many ATMs also offer the facility of depositing cash, providing information on balance in the customer's bank account and a few other ancillary services relating to their bank account. Thus, the currency notes can both enter an ATM from the hands of the public as well as exit from it into their hands.

The Journey Within the Economy

As may be seen from the above chain, the currency notes may come into the hands of the public and enter the economy at any stage from any or after all three destinations: from the currency chest branch, from the bank branch or from the ATM. In addition, a very few currency notes may come into the hands of the public directly from Reserve Bank of India as it also provides limited facilities of exchange of notes to members of the public.

Just like an individual's life, every currency note has its own life when it moves out from the security confines of the bank branch or an ATM into the big, outside world. There, it changes numerous hands, pockets and wallets and is treated differently by different people. Many notes may move between the public, bank branches and ATMs back and forth numerous times during the course of their life journey.

During the course of their life span, currency notes come across all sorts of people, from rich businessmen to politicians, from scholars to students, from farmers to small shopkeepers, from manual workers to even beggars. Indeed, if only the notes could speak, each one of them would have an interesting story to narrate about their lives and experiences during their journey within the economy!

Each individual note has its own active life-span, during which it remains in circulation. Notes which are treated well during their handling have a longer life span, while those which are subject to shabby or rough treatment have a shorter life span. During their active life-span, the notes are subjected to handling in all sorts of ways. These may get stored in neat and clean or unhygienic conditions. While some people take good care of the notes and keep them unfolded and straight, others may subject them to multiple folds and creases. Some people may use greasy, oily or dirty hands while handling the notes, subjecting them to stains and marks. Still others may even scribble some marks on the notes, thereby mistreating them.

During the course of this handling a multiple number of times, the paper of the notes gradually gets worn out and limp. The freshness and crackle that exists in a new note gradually gives way to limpness and softness in a much used note. Just as a person ages and wrinkles appear on her skin, so does a currency note gets aged with use. Just by looking at a currency note, one can make out the type of life it has led. Once the note gets so soiled and dirty and worn out that it is not fit to be exchanged further during the normal course of business, it is no longer issued further by a bank branch. It remains in the bank, being classified as a soiled note.

It may take a few months or some years for a note to get classified as a soiled note, depending upon its usage. A person may keep a fresh note in a box or cupboard for years before using it while another may use it immediately upon receiving it. It is generally believed that on an average, the life of a note is around one to two years. However, there would be very wide variations between individual notes.

Interestingly, how long is the lifespan of a currency note, on an average? According to expert opinion on the Gisecke+Devrient (top banknote printing and processing company) website, the lifespan of a banknote ranges between one and five years. How long it lasts only partly depends on how the public handle it – whether we use wallets or keep it loose in our pockets, for example. In fact, the wear and tear on banknotes continues throughout the cash cycle – from frequent sorting by automated systems, to ATM dispensing, to being passed on multiple times during our daily transactions. A banknote must meet various quality criteria to continue circulating. On the whole, the higher its value, the longer it can stay in circulation.[118]

The Return Journey

The return journey of currency notes begins when they get soiled, dirty or develop tears and cuts, and hence are no longer acceptable for transactions in the normal course. Such currency notes come to the bank branches in the receipts and get classified as soiled notes, that is, being not fit for reissuing to the public. These notes are segregated and stored separately as soiled notes in the vaults of banks.

Before the advent of Note Sorting Machines, this work of sorting the notes was done manually at bank branches, where cashiers had to sort the received currency notes into re-issuable and non-issuable (soiled) notes. With enormous increase in the quantity of notes in circulation over the years, the bank staff found it difficult to do this work.

The adoption of technology for sorting of currency notes commenced in 2004-05 with the Reserve Bank of India instructing currency chest branches of banks to install Note Sorting Machines. By 2007-08, all currency chest branches had installed Note Sorting

Machines.[119] These machines, besides counting the notes, sorted these into non-issuable (soiled) and issuable notes.

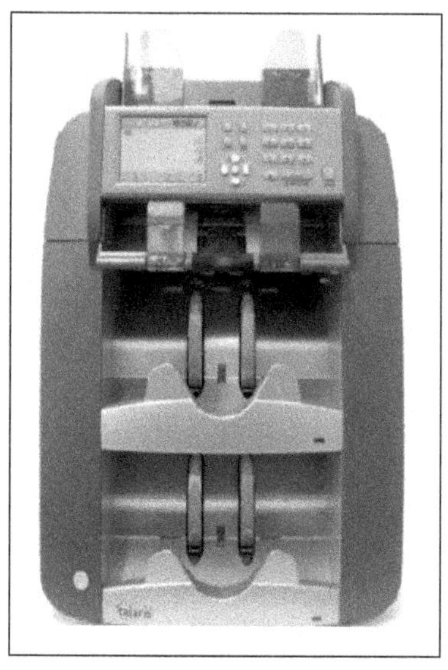

A Note Sorting Machine

Gradually, such machines came to be installed even at the other branches of banks. At present the Note Sorting Machines at banks perform this task of sorting the notes according to defined parameters. The notes which are classified as soiled notes are no longer to be issued to the public and kept separately for sending back to the Reserve Bank of India.

Just as the fresh notes move from the Reserve Bank of India to currency chests, the soiled notes move in the reverse direction, from currency chests to the Reserve Bank of India. Individual bank branches cannot send their soiled notes directly to the Reserve Bank of India. These branches must send the soiled notes to the currency chest branch with which they are linked, which consolidates notes received from all such branches at its end.

These soiled notes are then packed in boxes and despatched to the Reserve Bank of India as a soiled notes remittance, under police escort, with a representative of the currency chest accompanying the remittance. Just like a fresh notes remittance, the remittance of soiled notes is also received at the Issue Offices of the Reserve Bank of India. It is again here where the last scenes in the life cycle of currency notes are enacted.

Examination and Disposal

Just as notes are produced under tight security, their disposal has also to be done amidst adequate security, this time within the precincts of the Reserve Bank of India. The soiled notes received from currency chest branches are subjected to examination, verification and finally disposed in accordance with prescribed procedure.

Till the late 1990s, this process was done manually in the Reserve Bank of India through a battery of staff members, called Note Examiners. These Note Examiners would examine each note received for its genuineness and if found soiled, would certify it for final destruction. If certain notes were found to be still fit for circulation, these would be retrieved and spared from destruction. Any forged notes found would also be dealt with in accordance with prescribed procedures. The soiled notes would then be defaced by punching holes into them before being destroyed.

The process of destruction of notes was carried out manually by brick kiln and water-jacketed fire incinerators. The notes which were due for destruction were brought to the incinerator in gunny bags and put into the incinerator for being consigned to the flames. The process would produce a huge amount of smoke, toxic gases and ash into the atmosphere as the notes contain chemicals, pigments and colours.

The entire process of examination and disposal of notes was elaborate and time consuming and involved thousands of staff members. The work was done in a dusty and unhealthy environment and required close supervision at various stages. Thus, at the last stage of their life cycle, the notes were subjected to a lot of manual handling (and treated rather roughly) before these could meet their fiery end.

Winds of Change - Advent of Technology

The year 1998 marks a turning point in this story as it was then that the processes involved in handling of notes in the Reserve Bank of India underwent a drastic change. During the tenure of the then Governor, Dr Bimal Jalan, Reserve Bank of India embarked on a programme to mechanise its six-decade old currency examination, verification and destruction systems. The manual systems were sought to be replaced by sophisticated automated systems.

Work began as a pilot project and was subsequently extended to all the Issue Offices. By 2003, the hitherto existing dusty, noisy and unglamorous Note Examination and Verification Sections and the manual incineration systems in its Issue Offices were transformed and modernised.

The two machines instrumental in bringing about this transformation were the Currency Verification and Processing System (CVPS) and the Shredding and Briquetting System (SBS). Besides bringing standardisation to the entire process of note examination, it resulted in enormous increase in the note processing capacity. Environmental concerns and availability of secure technological options prompted the adoption of Shredding and Briquetting Systems for currency disposal.

The decades' long work procedures and practices gave way to an entirely new technology-driven system. From the perspective of the notes, as a result of this change, they could get benefits of lesser and smoother handling during the last stage of their existence!

Currency Verification and Processing System (CVPS)

CVPS is an electronic-mechanical device designed for examination, authentication, counting, sorting and online destruction of the notes which are unfit for further circulation. It is capable of sorting the notes on the basis of denomination, design and level of soilage. It sorts the notes into four categories, namely, Fit, Unfit, Reject and Suspect notes. The Unfit notes are shredded online. The Fit notes are retrieved and banded in packets of 100 pieces. Information such as denomination, date of processing, name of office, operator code is printed on the label to facilitate easy identification. The notes in the Reject and Suspect categories are collected in different stackers. These are to be inspected manually for the presence of counterfeit or different denomination notes.[120]

A Currency Verification and Processing System (CVPS) machine[121]

Any counterfeit notes detected during manual examination are dealt with in accordance with specified procedure. The unfit notes are kept separately and subjected to destruction in the off-line mode of Shredding and Briquetting System machines.

The CVPS ensures uniformity and consistency in the examination of notes on the basis of soilage levels and other parameters and classification thereof into re-issuable and non-issuable. The element of subjectivity, which characterised manual examination of notes, is eliminated through CVPS. The software of the system has the capability for gradation of access rights to it. This provides an element of electronic security apart from the regular security of the Issue

Offices. The system has a computer attached to capture and store the data as well as provide reports.[122]

Shredding and Briquetting System (SBS)

The SBS was introduced to replace the incineration of notes, which was not environment friendly. In SBS, the notes are put in the machine as such by way of bundles. The shredder first cuts the notes into small pieces and then converts them into fine shreds. These shreds are then automatically channelled into the Briquetting System where they are compressed under high pressure resulting into formation of briquettes. SBS are of two types, namely, on-line and off-line. The on-line systems accept the shreds of notes for briquetting both from its shredder as also from the CVPS. The off-line systems, however, accept shreds of notes for briquetting only from the shredder.[123]

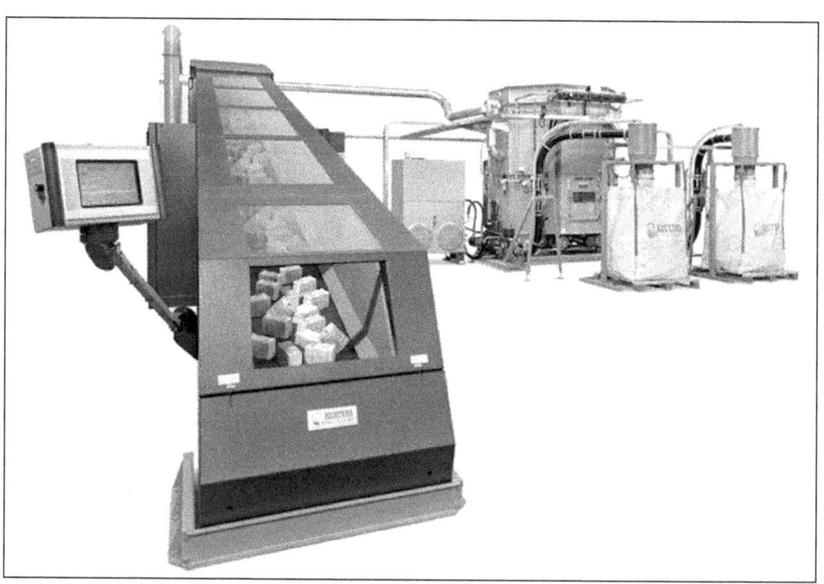

A Shredding and Briquetting System (SBS) machine[124]

The briquettes are cylindrical or brick-like in shape, approximately measuring 15 centimetres long and about 8.75 centimetres in diameter or 6 by 8.75 centimetres along the two other edges.

The journey of paper currency notes comes to an end when these once fresh, crisp notes now lie forlorn, converted as briquettes, stuffed into bags, awaiting disposal. The Reserve Bank of India finally disposes of these briquettes as waste to waste disposal contractors and companies. What a mundane end to such an eventful existence!

This waste material is most commonly used as landfills. However, there have been some novel instances where this waste material has also been put to good use. The items made from shredded currency include files, calendars and paper weights and ballpoint pen shells, tea coasters, cups and small trays, which are mainly used as souvenirs for guests. The technology for recycling old shredded notes was developed by the Nagpur-based National Environmental Engineering Research Institute.[125]

The Kumarappa National Handmade Paper Institute, Jaipur also developed a technology for converting shredded currency waste into good quality handmade paper. The handmade paper and board produced as a result of this technology was used to produce file covers, envelopes and other stationery items, which were supplied to various offices of the Reserve Bank of India and Khadi and Village Industries Commission.[126]

Interestingly, newspaper reports have mentioned that 800 tonnes of shredded currency briquettes were used by a plywood manufacturing unit in Kannur, Kerala. The shredded currency briquettes were mixed with wood chips to manufacture hardboards, which were then exported to South Africa and other countries.[127]

The CVPS and SBS machines have been upgraded periodically. The Reserve Bank of India is in the process of automating the process of banknote handling by inducting modern technology. A pilot project has already been initiated for this purpose. This is expected to automate receipt, storage, processing and destruction of banknotes; foster economies of scale; and make the currency management function more efficient.[128] This has become necessary with the growth in volume of banknotes in circulation in recent years. Between 2009-10 and 2019-20, the volume of banknotes in circulation doubled from 5,654.9 crore pieces to 11,597.7 crore pieces[129] (57 billion to 116 billion pieces approximately).

Endnote

The life journey of paper currency notes has changed markedly over the decades. With greater use of technology in the years to come, the process of handling of notes is going to get increasingly automated. Hopefully, the currency notes would get a more comfortable and fulfilling life-cycle as a result of these changes!

During the course of their life-journey, not all the notes pass through the above stages. During handling, some notes may be subjected to rough treatment. Some of these notes may get torn and bruised while others may lose certain portions. We may think that such notes have become worthless, but it may not be so. The next part of our story will deal with such cases: whether such notes can fetch any value, and if so, how much are these worth.

Chapter Six

Defective but Valued

During the course of its life cycle, with the passage of time, a currency note also grows old. From a crisp and crackling fresh note, it transforms into a soiled, dirty, torn or even mutilated note. Most notes become weak in the middle with constant folding and get torn vertically from the middle into two pieces. Sometimes, the note may even have a part thereof missing. In all such cases, the holder of such a note would not like to lose the value and prefer it to be exchanged with a fresh currency note. Fortunately, there are provisions for such exchange. This part of our story deals with rules for getting value for such defective notes. Over time, these rules have been simplified and are now quite clear and unambiguous. The infrastructure for providing facilities for such exchange has also been strengthened over the decades. At present, all bank branches are authorised to pay value for most of the types of defective notes to the public.

Just like any other product, currency notes also age with use as they change different hands, pockets and wallets. The note handling practices and etiquettes in the country are not conducive to their longevity as many persons do not carry wallets. Instead, they fold the notes multiple times and carry them in handkerchiefs or in the folds of their clothes. During the course of their life cycle, some notes may get subjected to excessive wear and tear. They may become extremely dirty, worn out, torn and cracked. There are other instances too which lead to damaging the notes during their life cycle.

For instance, some notes may get wet or washed, leading to crumpling and discolouration. There are instances, particularly in rural areas, when notes are kept buried in the ground in earthen pots or wooden boxes for safety and protection. In such circumstances, sometimes the notes may be damaged by moisture or termites. Such notes may have some portions thereof brittle or missing. During celebrations and festivals, there are practices of using currency notes as offering to deities. During such events, some notes may get stained, smeared with oil or partially burnt or charred and are in danger of deterioration with any further handling.

In all above types of cases, as well as otherwise too, the owners of defective or damaged notes would like to get value for the same. Fortunately, the Reserve Bank of India comes to the rescue of public in all such conditions. The following paragraphs of the story narrate how Reserve Bank of India has provided for payment of value to the genuine holders of defective notes, the different ways in which defective notes have been classified and the rules governing their payment.

Reserve Bank of India (Note Refund) Rules

The Reserve Bank of India Act, 1934 provides that no person shall of right be entitled to recover from the Central Government or the Bank, the value of any lost, stolen, mutilated or imperfect currency note, provided that the Bank may, with the previous sanction of the Central Government, prescribe the circumstances in and the conditions and limitations subject to which the value of such currency notes or bank notes may be refunded as of grace and the rules made shall be laid on the table of Parliament.[130] Further, the Central Board of the Bank has been empowered to make regulations under which value of such (lost, stolen, mutilated or imperfect) notes may be refunded.[131]

In accordance with the above provisions, the Reserve Bank of India has been framing the conditions under which the value of such defective notes may be paid. These are known as Note Refund Rules.

For the first time, Reserve Bank of India issued the RBI (Note Refund) Rules in 1935, based on the rules of the Paper Currency Department as they then stood.[132]

A new set of rules were issued in 1975, known as Reserve Bank of India (Note Refund) Rules, 1975. These Rules provided for powers to examine and dispose of the claims in respect of such damaged notes to be delegated to a number of officers at various levels. These Rules abolished the element of discretion previously vested in officers who were responsible for paying value in respect of defective notes. The objective was to facilitate the expeditious settlement of all genuine claims.

In these Rules, the distinctive number of the note (whether present in full or part thereof) presented for payment was of paramount importance for deciding whether the value for that note could be paid or not. In addition, the essential features present on the note, such as the signature of the Governor, the Ashoka Pillar emblem and the watermark were also taken into account for deciding the value to be paid.

With passage of time, it was felt that the Rules were still cumbersome to implement. These were again revised in 2009 as Reserve Bank of India (Note Refund) Rules, 2009. The emphasis in the revised rules was on the area of the note presented for payment rather than on the distinctive number of the note and its essential features. This simplified the interpretation and hence implementation of the Rules.

After the demonetisation of 2016, new notes of smaller size were introduced. Two new denominations, of ₹200 and ₹2,000 were also introduced. It, therefore, became necessary to amend the Rules, which was done in 2018. The amended Rules - which are in operation at present - are called Reserve Bank of India (Note Refund) Rules, 2009 [as Amended by Reserve Bank of India (Note Refund) Amendment Rules, 2018]. Commonly, these are referred to as NRR, 2009. These Rules provide for the terms and conditions under which such notes may be exchanged and their value paid.

Interestingly, while the Note Refund Rules have been amended several times over the years, the facility has all through been provided free of cost. There are no charges whatsoever levied on providing value to members of the public for this service. However, in legal terms, this facility is being provided not as a matter of right to the public but as a matter of grace.

Note Exchange 'Dealers'

Although a process for claiming value for such defective notes has existed ever since the Reserve Bank of India came into existence in 1935, as mentioned above, the procedures were not simple. Moreover, the infrastructure available was limited as, besides the Issue Offices of the Reserve Bank of India, only the designated currency chest branches (only with public sector banks) were authorised to exchange the defective notes. This had led to proliferation of thousands of note exchange 'dealers' all across the country, who catered to the need of the public for getting value for such defective notes. These shops or stalls generally came up at business centres and markets to exchange soiled and mutilated notes of the public and provide them with exchange value.

Stall of a dealer engaged in exchanging defective notes[133]

Of course, for their services, they charged a hefty commission. For example, a hundred rupee note, which was slightly damaged or a small portion of which was missing, would fetch only about thirty rupees or so at these shops while it would have got the full hundred rupees as per the Note Refund Rules.

Shortly after the Note Refund Rules were amended in 1975, the Reserve Bank of India had commented: "In view of the considerable volume of the circulation of currency and bank notes in India,...the comparatively small number of offices at which claims for the value of notes have been adjudicated so far and the limited delegation of powers under the rules,... a practice has also grown up, of members of the general public getting such notes exchanged through money changers and middlemen, who in the guise of charges for transport and other expenses incurred or services rendered by them, buy soiled and unserviceable notes at a discount, often in violation of Rule 128 of the Defence and Internal Security of India Rules, 1971, which prohibits any trading in currency notes or coins at a discount, and later on get them exchanged at various offices of the Reserve Bank of India."[134]

In addition to exchanging defective notes, many of these shops would also make available to the public fresh note packets of notes, mostly in the lower denominations at a premium to their actual value. There exists a huge market for new notes in India, which are often used as gifts in marriages and ceremonial occasions. These shops would cater to this demand of the public. In recent years, many of these shops have since downed shutters due to the spread of infrastructure for exchange of notes.

Spread of Infrastructure

In the initial decades, as mentioned above, only a limited number of bank branches (currency chests) were authorised to give value for defective notes. The fact of a bank branch being authorised to give value for defective notes was also never publicised. Thus, the public were in the dark about the availability of this facility to the common person. Although in 1997, the private sector banks maintaining currency chests were also authorised to give value for defective notes, the facility was available to a limited extent. The bank branches were also not proactive in providing this facility to the people as it entailed extra work for them. In 2004, Reserve Bank of India had to advise banks to provide this service to the public more actively and vigorously.[135]

However, the major change came about in 2013 when the Reserve Bank of India instructed that all bank branches (including those of cooperative banks and Regional Rural Banks) should provide the facility of exchange of cut/ mutilated notes to all members of public without discrimination on all working days. If a branch was unable to provide the service across the counter, it could accept the notes and send it to its linked currency chest and ensure value to the person within a reasonable time, say a fortnight.[136] This was an important milestone and paved the way for widespread availability of this facility to the public.

At present, the Reserve Bank of India has authorised all bank branches to provide such facilities on its behalf to members of the public in accordance with the Note Refund Rules. The Reserve Bank of India as well as banks has also been giving publicity to this measure through print and electronic media. This has now resulted in a much wider knowledge about this facility as compared to the past.

An advertisement released by the Reserve Bank of India, for educating the public regarding exchange of defective notes by bank branches

Categories of Defective Notes

Defective currency notes have been classified under various categories[137] such as soiled notes and mutilated notes, etc. These are described below:

- Soiled notes are the most common type of defective notes. As the name suggests, a soiled note is a note which has become dirty due to usage. However, in 1996-97, the definition of a soiled note was widened to include a two-piece note pasted together wherein both the pieces presented belong to the same note and form the entire note. Till then, such notes were included in the definition of mutilated notes.[138]

- Mutilated notes are those notes of which a portion is missing or which are composed of more than two pieces.
- Imperfect notes those which have been wholly or partially, obliterated, shrunk, washed, altered or indecipherable but does not include a mutilated note.
- A mismatched note is a note which has been formed by joining a half note of any one note to a half note of another note. A mismatched note can be identified on the basis of number, signature etc. and /or after examining other security features.
- Extremely brittle, badly burnt, charred or inseparably stuck up notes (due to conditions such as fire or termites) which cannot withstand further handling or which may lose their original identity with the passage of time.

At present, the Rules prescribe that the facility for exchange of soiled, mutilated and imperfect notes is to be provided by all banks at all their branches. The liberalised definition of soiled note to include two-piece notes resulted in classifying most of the defective notes as soiled notes.

Reserve Bank of India has instructed banks to accept soiled notes for exchange over their counters in payment of Government dues and for credit to accounts of the public maintained with banks. However, in no case, these notes should be issued back to the public. These notes have to be deposited in currency chests for onward transmission to Reserve Bank of India offices as soiled note remittances for further processing.[139]

Payment of Value for Different Types of Notes

Although a first reading of the rules in regard to payment of value for defective notes may look to daunting, the present rules are quite simple to understand. Even a common person, sitting at home, can know the value that would be payable on a defective note in his or her possession. This section describes these rules in simple language. For better understanding and clarity, a few illustrations are also given.

Interestingly, up to 2009, the focus of the Note Refund Rules while deciding about the payment in respect of a defective note was on the distinctive number/s printed on the note. The presence of the number/s, or at least the major part of the number/s, was instrumental in deciding the value payable in respect of the note. Without the presence of the distinctive number/s of the note, no value could be paid. If only one of the two numbers (where the numbers appeared at two places) was available, full value could not be paid for the note. All that changed when the Note Refund Rules were amended in 2009. The focus shifted to the area of the largest piece of the note presented for payment. When the Rules were again amended in 2018, the focus on the area continued. At present, for example, the holder of a defective note of ₹2,000, even with both distinctive numbers missing, is entitled to full value for the note, if the single undivided area presented for payment is more than 80 per cent of the total area of the note.

The payment of value of a defective note would depend upon the type of note as per its classification and its specific condition. The Rules provide that all soiled notes are payable for full face value: for example, a soiled note of ₹50 would be paid a value of ₹50. It is reiterated that a note that is torn into two pieces and the pieces are pasted together, is now defined as a soiled note.

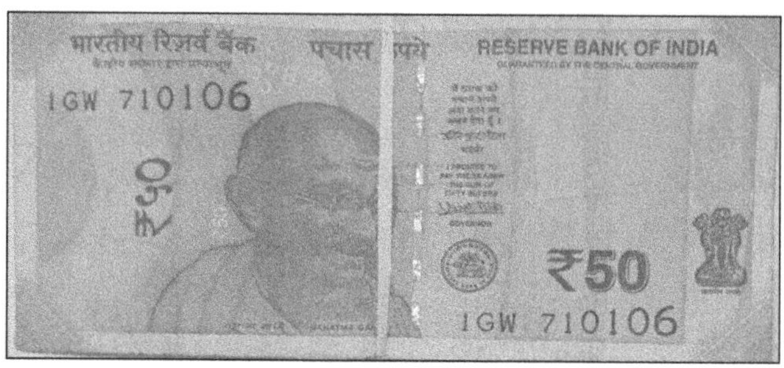

A ₹50 note, torn at the centre in two pieces and pasted is payable for full value (₹50) as it is classified as a soiled note. This is the most common form of defective note.

As regards other types of defective notes, the area of the piece of the note presented for payment as a percentage of the total area of the note is the determining factor for the value payable for the note. Sometimes, the area can be guessed by simply looking at the note. When there is a doubt, the area can be measured by using a transparent plastic plate, on which a centimetre grid is printed. The area would be determined by counting the number of complete squares available on largest available undivided piece of the note.

The precise rules for payment of value of different categories of notes, are described below.[140]

- Mutilated notes of ₹1, 2, 5, 10 and 20 denomination: If the area of the single largest undivided piece of the note presented is more than 50 per cent of the area of the respective denomination, rounded off to the next complete square centimetre, full value of the note shall be payable. If the area of the largest undivided piece of the note presented is less than or equal to 50 per cent of the area of the note, no value shall be paid. Specific details, denomination-wise, of actual area of notes and the minimum area required for payment of full value are given in Appendix IV.

- Mutilated notes of ₹50, 100, 200 and 2,000 denomination: If the area of the single largest undivided piece of note is more than 80 per cent of the area of the respective denomination rounded off to the next complete square centimetre, full value of the note shall be payable. If the undivided area of the single largest undivided piece of the note is equal to or more than 40 per cent and less than or equal to 80 per cent of the area of the respective denomination rounded off to the next complete square centimetre, half the value of the note is payable. If the area of the single largest undivided piece of the note is less than 40 per cent, no value shall be payable. If the note presented consists of two pieces of the same note and the two pieces, individually have an area equal to or more than 40 percent of the total area of the note in that denomination, then full value of the note shall be payable. Specific details, denomination-wise, of actual area of notes and the minimum area required on the single largest piece of note for payment of full value or half value, are given in Appendix IV.
- Mismatched notes: In case of notes up to ₹20 denomination, the area of the larger of the two pieces presented may be measured and value given as per rules for mutilated notes. If none of the two pieces presented meets the minimum area stipulated as per the provisions for mutilated notes, no value should be paid. In case of ₹50 and above denominations, the two pieces may be treated as two separate entities and dealt with accordingly.
- Imperfect notes: These notes may be paid for full value/ half value as specified for mutilated notes, if the matter, which is printed on the note has not become totally illegible and the Prescribed Officer is satisfied, having regard to the printed matter which is legible on the note, that it is a genuine note.
- Extremely brittle, burnt up, charred or stuck up notes: Such notes are required to be submitted to the Issue Department

of Reserve Bank of India for payment. If the notes can withstand handling through post, these can be sent by post or dropped in the special receptacle kept at offices of the RBI. However, if the notes are such that they could be further damaged by sending as such, the same can also be brought personally to the Issue Department. The adjudication of these notes is done by a team of officers of the Reserve Bank of India in the presence of the person who has tendered the notes or his/ her representative.

A ₹500 mutilated note in three pieces, with the largest piece having area of more than 40 per cent and less than 80 per cent, is payable for half value (₹250)

A ₹100 mutilated note with lower right number missing, payable for full value (₹100) as the area of largest piece is over 80 per cent of the total area of the note

A ₹2,000 mutilated note in four parts, not payable for any value as area of the largest piece is less than 40 per cent of the area of the note

A ₹20 mutilated note in four pieces, payable for full value (₹20) as the area of single largest piece is more than 50 per cent of the area of the note

A ₹2,000 mutilated note with both numbers missing, but still payable for full value (₹2,000) as the area of the largest piece is more than 80 per cent of the total area of the note

A ₹5 mutilated note with portion missing but payable for full value (₹5) as area of single largest piece presented is more than 50 per cent of the total area of the note

A ₹100 mismatched note with different numbers, payable for half value (₹50) as the larger piece presented is more than 40 per cent but less than 80 per cent of the total area of the note and the smaller piece is less than 40 per cent of the total area of the note

Notes Which Cannot Be Paid

While generally the payment of value of defective notes is governed by the rules given above, all defective notes which satisfy the area criteria as mentioned in the above paragraphs are not eligible for payment of value. The Note Refund Rules provide for certain categories of notes for which payment shall not be made. These include[141]:

- allegedly stolen, lost or wholly destroyed notes;
- notes, for which value has already been paid or which have been cancelled by RBI;

- notes which cannot be identified with certainty as a genuine;
- notes which have been deliberately cut, torn, defaced, altered or dealt with in any other manner for making of a false claim;
- notes carrying any extrinsic words or visible representations capable of conveying any message of a political or religious character or furthering the interest of any person or entity;
- notes which have been imported into India from any place outside India in contravention of the provision of any law;
- if any information called by the Prescribed Officer is not furnished by the claimant within a period of three months; and
- if a deliberate fraudulent intention appears in respect of a claim.

In the above provisions, the most important one is about the genuineness of the note. The official making the payment has to be satisfied that the note for which payment is being made is a genuine note. For this purpose, the official can rely on the essential features of the note, as given[142] in the Note Refund Rules.

Essential features means the features, including security features, which are necessary for the identification of a note, namely, the name of the issuing authority in Hindi and/or English; the guarantee clause in Hindi and/or in English; the promise clause in Hindi and/or in English; the signature in Hindi and/or in English; the Ashoka Pillar emblem or Mahatma Gandhi portrait, as the case may be; and the water-mark of the Ashoka Pillar emblem or Mahatma Gandhi portrait, as the case may be.

For this purpose, the security features of a note, for deciding the genuineness or otherwise, include, paper quality; size and shape of numbers; security thread; intaglio printing; latent image in vertical band; electrotype watermark (in watermark window); micro lettering; fluorescence (number panels and central band); Optically Variable Ink; see-through Register, and any other security feature that may be introduced by the Reserve Bank of India.

The officer responsible for paying the value in respect of defective notes is vested with necessary powers in this regard to make payment in accordance with the prescribed rules.

Procedural Aspects[143]

- For exchange of soiled notes: For up to 20 pieces of soiled notes presented by a person per day, with a maximum value of ₹5,000 per day, banks should exchange them over the counter, free of charge. If the number of notes or value exceeds the above limits, banks may accept them, against receipt, for value to be credited later; in such cases, banks can levy service charges for providing this service. This has been done so that banks are able to provide better customer service and to ensure that the facility is not cornered by a few.
- For exchange of mutilated notes: Where the number of notes presented by a person is up to 5 pieces, non-chest branches should normally pay the exchange value over the counter. If the number of notes presented exceeds 5 pieces with value not exceeding ₹5,000, the person should be advised to send such notes to nearby currency chest branch by insured post or get them exchanged thereat in person. All other persons tendering mutilated notes with value exceeding ₹5,000 should be advised to approach nearby currency chest branch.
- Time limit: Every effort should be made to pay the exchange value in minimum possible time, but in any case, it should be on the same day.[144] Currency chest branches receiving mutilated notes through post should credit the exchange value to the account of sender by electronic means within 30 days of their receipt.

The procedure for providing value to the members of public in exchange for defective notes has been made quite simple and people-friendly. It has been the endeavour of the Reserve Bank of

India that genuine people who come into possession of defective notes get this facility nearer to their doorstep and without payment of any charges.

Endnote

Over the decades, there has been a vast improvement in the facilities available to the public for payment of value in respect of the defective notes that they may come to possess. However, given the vast expanse of the country and the limited penetration of banking facilities, more needs to be done. Public awareness, regarding the facilities available to them as per the prescribed rules, also needs to be augmented.

From defective notes, our story will now move towards another interesting area. The quality of notes in circulation in the economy has been a focus area for the Reserve Bank of India for the last twenty five years. In the next phase of our story, we will recount the initiatives taken by it in maintaining the quality of notes, through what has been called its Clean Note Policy.

Chapter Seven

Quest for Quality

Today, we are used to seeing and using good quality clean notes in our day-to-day transactions. But it was not always so. Old timers would recall the period in the 1970s and 1980s when the quality of currency notes in the market was quite poor. Cut, torn, pasted and damaged notes, especially in the lower denominations, were widely used for transactions. It was only towards the end of 1990s that this scenario began to change. The Clean Note Policy of the Reserve Bank of India was behind this. This part of our story deals with the initiatives taken by the central bank over the years to improve the quality of currency notes in circulation in the country. Notable among these were increased printing capacity of notes, adoption of technology for processing and destruction of notes, de-stapling of note packets, simplification of Note Refund Rules and attempting to improve awareness of the bankers and the public.

Good quality currency notes play an important role in projecting a positive image of the nation. People prefer to hold on to crisp, clean notes and do not want to keep notes that are dirty, damaged or defaced. People would rather use the dirty notes first so as to get them out of their wallets at the earliest; this further increases the rate of deterioration of these notes!

Moreover, dirty and worn out notes significantly diminish the effect of security features present therein; hence it becomes difficult to identify whether the note that you possess is genuine or counterfeit. In today's world, when cash handling is getting increasingly automated, clean notes enhance the efficiency of the cash cycle as automated handling in ATMs and cash processing systems is improved with fewer jams and disruptions.

It is for the central bank of the country to ensure the quality of notes in circulation. The Reserve Bank of India Act, 1934 casts upon the Bank to maintain the quality of notes in the country: according to Section 27 of the Act, the Bank shall not re-issue banknotes which are torn, defaced or excessively soiled.

Poor Condition of Notes

Clean notes are taken for granted in today's monetary transactions. The public is reluctant to handle a currency note which has even a slight hairline tear. But it was not so, not so long ago. Cut back to thirty years: old-timers would recall that the market was full of dirty, soiled, worn-out, torn and pasted notes, which were being used freely as a medium of exchange. It was necessitated by circumstances, as there were few good quality currency notes available in the market. Good, clean notes were the crying need of the times. The decades of 1970s, 1980s and 1990s were characterised by shortage of currency notes, thereby leading to the poor quality of notes in circulation.

During these decades, data shows that the currency in circulation increased rapidly. While the year-on-year growth rate during 1971-80 was 11.9 per cent, it rose to 14.6 per cent during 1981-90 and further to 15.2 per cent in 1991-2000.[145] The currency in circulation grew from Rs 4,557 crore in 1970-71 to Rs 175,846 crore in 1998-99.[146] That was a growth of nearly 39 times during 28 years. Moreover, between 1978 and 1987, the hundred rupee note was the highest available denomination of currency, the higher denominations having been demonetised.

While various reasons could be attributed to explain the phenomenal growth in note issue, certain factors stand out: large expansion of the economy requiring greater use of cash, continuing public preference for currency notes as a medium of exchange and growth of population.

The increase in note issue was not matched by a proportionate increase in the infrastructure for producing currency notes. By the 1970s and 1980s, the quality of currency notes in the economy had deteriorated considerably. Cut, torn, pasted, worn out and damaged notes were being used in transactions. The situation was extremely bad in the case of notes in the lower (Rupee One, Two and Five) denominations. These notes, which accounted for the highest percentage of notes (more than 60 per cent) in circulation, were the most quickly soiled and damaged.

As a result of this shortage, the notes available had to remain in circulation in the economy far longer than their normal life span. The Reserve Bank of India took up the matter with the Government of India at the highest level but there was not much improvement in the supply position.

The third volume of the history of the Reserve Bank of India, dealing with the years 1967 to 1981, has devoted nine full pages to describing the shortage of supply of currency notes from the printing presses and the precarious position of quality of currency in the economy during those years. It states that during this period, the Reserve Bank of India had to function in an environment of short supply of notes, particularly in the lower denomination notes. Due to inadequate supply of fresh notes from the presses, it had to severely curtail the note supply to its offices and the currency chests and also issue instructions to salvage maximum number of re-issuable notes.[147] The curtailed supply of fresh notes as well as re-issuing the poor quality notes by banks resulted in growing resentment and criticism from the public.

Interestingly, in a letter written by Governor, S. Jagannathan to the Finance Minister, Y.B. Chavan on October 9, 1973 regarding the acute shortage of notes, a letter received from a disgruntled member of the public was enclosed to highlight the problem, for which the country's central bank was being blamed. The enclosed letter read:

The Reserve Bank Governor
Bombay-1

Damn Your

You and your officers deserve to be shot dead for your bungling. For our convenience we bank our money in nearby banks. They give me soiled and torn notes. They say the money has been got from Reserve Bank. So they won't give good notes. If we go to shop or hotel, we cannot exchange the notes for our necessities. What the hell do you want me to do with the notes? Neither the bank which gave me would accept them nor shopkeepers. So we have to come all the way to your stupid office and wait in queue? Why the hell can't you withdraw old notes at source itself, i.e. in your office itself. For your mismanagement, you should be given a garland of torn notes.

Sd: N. Akhileshwar[148]

Initial Measures Taken

The Government of India as well as the Reserve Bank of India has taken various steps to address the problem of shortage of currency and also the deteriorating quality of notes in circulation over a period of time. The initial measures taken to alleviate the problem commenced with setting up of a new currency note printing press at Dewas in Madhya Pradesh in 1974. Notes in the denomination of Rupees Twenty and Fifty were introduced in 1975 to reduce the pressure on notes of Rupees Ten. A new metallic rupee was introduced in 1975 to supplement the availability and stocks of one-rupee notes. Subsequently, Rupees Two and Five notes were also gradually coinised.[149]

In 1980, the Government was hopeful that, with the introduction of a second shift at the Dewas press and some improvements at the Nasik press, the demand for notes could be met in the next four to five years.[150] But that was not to be. The position continued to remain acute throughout the decade.

In order to overcome the acute shortage of notes in the country, the installed capacity for printing of fresh notes and the production of bank note paper was substantially increased. The existing currency note printing presses at Nasik and Dewas were modernised. Two new printing presses with the state-of-art technology were set up at Mysore and Salboni. To bridge the demand-supply gap, 3.6 billion pieces of notes were imported during 1997-98. It was only by 1999-2000 when enough printing capacity was installed in the country to take care of the current and foreseeable future requirements of currency.

Apart from augmenting the supply of fresh notes in the economy, the withdrawal of soiled and mutilated notes from circulation was equally important. Simultaneously, Reserve Bank of India increased the number of note examination sections and staff employed for the examination of soiled and mutilated notes so that the excessively soiled and defective notes could be removed from circulation as expeditiously as possible. In spite of these efforts, the claims in respect of soiled and mutilated notes rose by leaps and bounds and the quality of notes in circulation continued to deteriorate. It was no more possible to handle these claims manually and maintain the quality of notes in circulation at the desired level by using the prevailing methods and techniques of currency management.[151]

Introduction of New Technology

Hence it was no more a choice, but an imperative to bring the methods and techniques of currency management in consonance with new technology and international best practices. Accordingly, Dr. Bimal Jalan, the then Governor, Reserve Bank of India announced the Bank's 'Clean Note Policy' in January 1999.[152] The objective of the policy was to provide the citizens good quality currency notes while withdrawing the soiled notes out of circulation. While the supply side issues had been taken care of by that time, the quantum of soiled notes in the economy was a cause of concern.

The Reserve Bank of India introduced modern technology in its staid and old-fashioned Issue Offices to increase its note processing capacity. These included the mechanisation of note examination and destruction processes. This was done by installing Currency Verification and Processing System (CVPS) machines[153] in the Issue Department. A single Currency Verification and Processing System (CVPS) machine could process over 50,000 notes per hour as against about 3,000 notes per person per day in the manual system. By 2003, Reserve Bank of India had 48 of such machines installed in its Issue Offices.[154]

The other machines that revolutionised the note destruction process in the Reserve Bank of India were the Shredding and Briquetting System (SBS) machines.[155] These machines, either in combination with the CVPS machines or on a stand-alone basis, ensured the destruction of soiled notes without manual intervention. Moreover, these were environmental friendly machines unlike the earlier procedures which required burning of notes and created smoke and ash. By 2004, 27 SBS machines had been installed in the 18 Issue Offices of the Reserve Bank of India.[156]

Deputy Governor Vepa Kamesam, who was in-charge of the currency management function in the Reserve Bank of India from

July 2001 to September 2003, steered the Clean Note Policy in its initial years with a missionary zeal and some unconventional ways. Under his stewardship, these two sets of machines transformed the decades' old systems of note processing and destruction in the Reserve Bank of India in a way that was simply unthinkable a few years ago.

Interestingly, the re-engineering of work processes due to technological changes in the area of currency management had another fall out. The Reserve Bank of India was faced with surplus staff, which led to the introduction of an Optional Early Retirement Scheme during 2003. Under the scheme, employees who had completed 25 years of service and were at least 50 years old were given the option to retire voluntarily. As many as 4,468 employees, comprising 15.8 per cent of the work force, availed of the scheme.[157] Due to this scheme as well as normal retirements, the Reserve Bank of India became a much leaner institution. Between December 2002 and December 2004, it had shed 6,157 employees: the total staff strength declined from 28,884 to 22,727.[158]

The total disposal of soiled notes, which was 5.1 billion pieces during 2000-01[159] rose to 10.6 billion pieces in 2001-02 and further to 15.6 billion pieces in 2002-03.[160] It resulted in an enormous release of precious space in the vaults of the currency chests and enabled the banks to mop up soiled notes from the system. This level could only be surpassed over a decade later, during 2015-16 when 16.4 billion pieces of soiled notes were disposed off.[161]

Soiled Notes Redefined and Sunday Exchange

Another impediment in note processing was the enormous volume of mutilated notes in the system, which had to be adjudicated and whose value needed to be paid in accordance with the Note Refund Rules. Most of these notes were torn at the middle and in two pieces, pasted by tape. In 1996-97, the definition of a soiled note was liberalised to include two-piece notes, where both pieces belonged to the same note, to be classified as a soiled note.[162] This reduced the load on the note adjudication system in banks and the Reserve Bank of India as most of the notes which had to go through the adjudication process earlier could now be accepted by the banks and exchanged in the normal course of business.

During 2000-01, the Reserve Bank of India and the currency chest branches settled claims with respect to mutilated notes under the Note Refund Rules involving 405 lakh pieces as compared with 516 lakh pieces in 1999-2000. The decline was, *inter alia*, due to the above decision as a large number of such notes were exchanged across the counters of banks.[163]

Another measure which contributed to reduce the extent of soiled notes in the system was taken towards late 2002, when the Reserve Bank of India, on an experimental basis, requested banks to open one currency chest branch on one Sunday in a month at selected centres to exclusively provide currency exchange and distribute small coins to the public. Banks reported that the experiment received tremendous response from the public. It was then decided that banks should run this scheme on a permanent basis with whole-hearted participation. The choice of the centre and the Sunday in the month was left to the individual bank to decide.

Discontinuing Stapling of Notes and Writing on Watermark

A major factor causing damage to currency notes, and consequently reducing their life span, was the practice of stapling the note packets at the left edge, which had been continuing for several decades. The new currency notes issued by the printing presses had a staple to secure a note packet (of 100 pieces). During the course of their handling by banks and the public, the notes were subjected to stapling again and again. As a result, the notes bore multiple holes and got damaged and torn in that area. This practice was the subject of numerous complaints and even ridicule.

Interestingly, in an article on the decision to do away with stapling of note packets, the Financial Express quoted an excerpt from traveller Matt Donath's 'Round The World Journal' (Part 12: 'Tea Break in Darjeeling'), where he comments on the condition of notes in India as well the practice of stapling of note packets. He writes, "One of my sick day tasks is to remove the staples from the wad of 100 rupee notes Sybil picked up at the bank. India has a bizarre currency situation, with few large or small denomination bills. Consequently, you have to carry large wads of 100 rupee notes and many people can't make small change. Since small bills haven't been printed for years, any you see are on the verge of disintegration. Insanely, in order to transport all the 100 rupee notes, banks use huge staples to wad them together in groups of one hundred. Our wad had about 8 staples through it from either side. Worse, the staples get bent and twisted into each other, creating a Chinese puzzle when you attempt to remove them. The task is greatly complicated by the fact that many of the bills have been stapled together so many times that large holes form in them."[164]

A study conducted by the Reserve Bank of India found that no other country followed the practice of stapling of notes. The Government and the Reserve Bank of India, therefore, decided to do away with the stapling of notes.[165] The process was initiated in 1996. The note presses supplying fresh notes gave up stapling the notes and started putting plastic bands to secure the packets. Some years later, they were replaced by paper bands.

Fresh note packets with staples

In 1996, the Reserve Bank of India issued advice to all banks to stop stapling fresh note packets and in 1998 the instructions were reiterated in the case of re-issuable notes.[166] But there was little effect and banks had to be reminded repeatedly to give effect to the instructions. But it was very difficult to get them to break the decades' long practice.

In November 2001, the Reserve Bank of India had to issue a directive in public interest to all banks prohibiting stapling of bank notes, requiring the tendering of soiled notes to the Reserve Bank in unstapled condition and the issue of only clean notes to the public.[167] Initially, banks did not evince keen interest in implementing the provisions of the directive. Added to this, some trade unions in the banking industry had a few misgivings about the new dispensation, mainly on the grounds of security considerations and possible retrenchment of labour.[168]

Further, to ensure compliance, RBI instructed banks that their currency chests should hold their balance only in unstapled condition and the amount of stapled note balances should be treated as non-chest balance. During inspection of currency chests by Reserve Bank of India, the inspectors were asked to verify compliance with these instructions and penalties were imposed on banks for non-compliance. By end of July 2003, most of the currency chests had complied with the provisions in respect of notes lying in their vaults.

But there were occasional lapses. In March 2004, Bimal Jalan, after his retirement (as Governor, Reserve Bank of India) was given a stapled bundle of currency notes by a bank branch in New Delhi.[169]

Another irritating practice in vogue was the writing on the watermark of the currency note, which was largely adopted by banks while dealing with cash transactions. Besides disfiguring the watermark impression and rendering it difficult for easy recognition, this also created difficulties when the notes were being passed through note sorting machines as any mark appearing on the watermark of the note would render it to be classified as a non-issuable note. The Reserve Bank of India issued a directive in November 2001 advising banks to stop writing of any kind on the watermark window of bank notes.

By 2004-05, there was a marked improvement in the quality of notes in circulation due to the various measures taken.[170] But alas! Old habits die hard. The efforts taken on war footing had turned the tide and the worst was over. But these needed to be sustained on a regular basis.

Years later, instances of stapling and writing on the watermark portion of the notes were still coming to notice. Again, in May 2013, Reserve Bank of India had to reiterate that banks should not staple any note packet and instead secure them with paper bands; sort notes into re-issuables and non-issuables, and issue only clean notes to public; and stop writing of any kind on watermark window of bank notes.[171] Thankfully, the stapling of notes has now been consigned to history though instances of scribbling and marking on notes are still observed.

Note Sorting Machines

Before the advent of Note Sorting Machines, the sorting of notes into re-issuables (those that can be issued to the public) and non-issuables (those that were not fit for further circulation) was being done manually in banks. But with growing volume of notes in circulation, this work could not be done properly by the limited staff and was being neglected. Luckily, technology for carrying out this voluminous task was now available. In 2004, Reserve Bank of India advised the banks, initially the currency chest branches, to install Note Sorting Machines for sorting of the notes. By 2007-08, all currency chest branches had installed Note Sorting Machines. Within a few years, most bank branches were equipped with such machines.

This measure speeded up the tedious process of seeing each note manually and sorting it into re-issuable or non-issuable categories. In 2010-11, banks were advised to ensure that all notes received by them were processed before re-issuing them to the public. This was done to ensure that no soiled notes, which are received in the bank branches, are issued back to the public.

In 2010, Reserve Bank of India prescribed the parameters and standards to which these machines should conform so that these are able to check the authenticity and fitness of notes.[172] This brought a measure of standardisation to the process of note sorting as the machines sorted the notes on the basis of pre-defined criteria. As new series of notes have been introduced since then, these parameters have been revised in 2022.[173]

Little Impact on Lower Denominations

Despite all these measures, the objective of the Clean Note Policy could not be fully achieved even by 2014. In a speech given by K.C. Chakraborty, then Deputy Governor of Reserve Bank of India, he admitted that while the objectives of Clean Note Policy had been by and large achieved in respect of higher denomination notes, the quality of lower denomination notes, especially ₹10, continued to be a cause for concern, possibly due to reluctance/constraints on the part of banks to mop up such notes from circulation.[174]

During the four year period between 2010-11 and 2013-14, soiled notes in the ₹10 denomination formed between 26.1 and 28.9 per cent of the total soiled notes disposed; however, the share of ₹10 denomination notes in the total notes in circulation was between 33 and 34.4 per cent.[175] These figures explain the concern expressed above, as lesser percentage of ₹10 notes were disposed off during that period.

A rough measure of the quality of notes in circulation is the time span in which the currency notes are replaced after being in use. This can be calculated by dividing the total notes in circulation by the disposal of soiled notes during the year. For example, the notes in circulation as at the end of March 2007 were 39.8 billion while during 2006-07, 7.3 billion soiled notes were disposed. It means that for the entire number of notes to be replaced (at the same rate of disposal), it would have taken about 5.5 years.

However, the above figures were for all denominations taken together. If granular denomination-wise figures are studied, these would give different values for each denomination. To continue with the example, for the same period, if the data for ₹10 notes is considered, it shows that it would have taken just 3.3 years to replace this denomination, as number of ₹10 notes was 7.2 billion while the ₹10 notes disposed were 2.2 billion.

If similar data for 2013-14 are considered, it is found that for all the denominations, the time period for replacement worked out to 5.4 years, which is almost the same as for the earlier period. However, for the ₹10 denomination, the time period for replacement worked out to 6.5 years. It showed that the ₹10 notes were remaining in circulation for a much longer time, hence they were in rather bad condition. Generally speaking, the lower denomination notes get soiled at a quicker rate as compared to the higher denomination notes.

Withdrawal of Old Series of Notes and Demonetisation

Another measure taken under the Clean Note Policy was the withdrawal of old series of notes, printed prior to 2005. Notes printed prior to 2005 did not have the year of printing mentioned thereon; it was only in that year when the year of printing of the note started appearing on the reverse side of the note. In 2014, Reserve Bank of India decided that all old series of banknotes issued prior to 2005 will be completely withdrawn from circulation, although these would continue to be legal tender. It was stated that such notes (issued prior to 2005) would be acceptable for monetary transactions only till March 31, 2014. Thereafter, the public will be required to approach bank branches, which would provide them exchange facilities on an ongoing basis.

In March, 2014, banks were advised that such notes should be exchanged freely from all members of the public, whether customers or non-customers. The service was to be provided free of cost. No restrictions were to be placed regarding the number of notes to be exchanged by a person. Further, banks were not to issue such notes across their counters or through ATMs.[176] The period up to which these notes could be exchanged at bank branches was extended several times lastly up to June 30, 2016. After that date, such notes could be exchanged only at the Issue Offices of the Reserve Bank of India.

In a way, the demonetisation of high denomination notes carried out in 2016 also contributed to the Clean Note Policy as notes in the denominations of 500 and 1,000 were withdrawn from circulation and were replaced by new notes in denominations of 500 and 2,000. Subsequently, new notes in other denominations were also issued. Gradually, the old series of notes are now getting reduced.

In May 2023, the Reserve Bank of India decided that the 2,000-rupee denomination notes should be withdrawn from circulation as these had completed their estimated lifespan. These notes, however, continue to be legal tender. Holders of these notes can get value for the same by tendering them at any of the Issue Offices of Reserve Bank of India as per procedure prescribed.

Increasing Awareness

After the enunciation of the Clean Note Policy, the Reserve Bank of India has taken steps to educate the public about the importance of proper handling of notes. An awareness campaign was launched to educate the public about not writing on the watermark window of notes, not folding the notes and not stapling the notes.

In 2001-02, the Reserve Bank of India set up a 'Currency Link' on its website, covering various aspects related to Indian currency and frequently asked questions (FAQs) and press releases on the subject. In 2002-03, it launched a publicity campaign on the benefits of non-stapling of notes through films and press advertisements.

In 2005, the Monetary Museum - the first of its kind in the country - was set up adjacent to the Reserve Bank of India office in Mumbai to preserve the country's monetary heritage and depict the history of currency and the evolution of money in India. However, much more needs to be done in a country where note handling practices are far from conducive to their health and well being.

The ultimate onus of having good quality, clean notes in the economy is upon the public who handle currency notes every day of their lives. For it is during the day-to-day handling of notes that they get subjected to wear and tear and suffer all kinds of bruises and damages. It is important that the people are sensitised to careful handling of currency. Our currency deserves much more respect and care than it actually receives.

Endnote

We have come a long way since worn out and pasted notes were being used freely in the economy. Now, we are used to handling reasonably clean and crisp currency. With increasing mechanisation of currency handling procedures, the sorting and weeding out of soiled currency will become even more standardised in the years ahead. If handling of currency by the public is further improved, our notes would be in better shape for longer duration.

From clean notes, our story now moves on to counterfeit notes. The next chapter will address the menace of counterfeit currency, its prevalence and the legal provisions to deal with the same. It will also narrate the procedure prescribed for dealing with counterfeit notes detected during the course of our daily transactions.

Chapter Eight

Countering Counterfeits

The problem of counterfeit notes is as old as the existence of paper money. On their part, the issuers of currency notes regularly take measures to make their currency notes secure and difficult to copy. These include using special quality of paper, sophisticated methods of printing and building in security features which are difficult to replicate. The designs of currency notes are also changed at periodical intervals. Still, counterfeiters manage to thrive. Every year, the Reserve Bank of India and the National Crime Records Bureau report the details of number of counterfeit notes detected in the banking channel and seized by law-enforcement agencies respectively. Possession and dealing with counterfeit notes is unlawful and invites punishment under the Indian Penal Code, 1860. The Reserve Bank of India also educates the public about the security features of currency notes to help them to distinguish between a genuine and a fake note.

Who doesn't want to get rich quickly? The temptation to counterfeit money has been prevalent throughout history so much so that it is sometimes called the world's "second oldest profession". All issuers of currency notes have had to deal with the challenge of duplicates of notes coming into circulation. Currency notes, and before that coins, have been subjected to counterfeiting for as long as they have existed.

In 13th century China, when paper money was introduced, counterfeiters were punished with death. One of the early currency notes of that period contains this stern admonition at the bottom: "Counterfeiters will be put to death; those who report counterfeiters to authorities will be awarded 5 *zhen* silver, along with the family property of the counterfeiters."[177]

Early Period

The early issuers of currency - individual banks - which had a limited circulation of their currency, almost crashed when faced with news of forgeries of their currency notes. In 1819, the erstwhile Bank of Hindostan, (which had its own currency notes) experienced a run following a notice issued by the bank pointing out how to distinguish genuine from forged notes.[178] In 1848, the erstwhile Bank of Bombay (which too had its own currency notes) experienced a run when some forged notes were discovered. Between November 7-14, 1848, its notes in circulation fell from Rs 51.65 lakh to Rs 25.46 lakh.[179]

Even during the period when currency notes were being issued by Government of India, cases of forgeries continued to be reported. The first set of British India notes, called the Victoria Portrait series, had to be withdrawn in the wake of a spate of forgeries.[180] Data reveals that that the number of forged notes received at Currency Offices was 19 in 1892-93, 155 in 1900 and 100 in 1905. These increased to 1,174 notes in 1919 and to 14,160 notes in 1925.[181]

The menace of forged notes continued even after the notes issue function was taken over by the Reserve Bank of India in 1935. Since the very beginning, every year, the Reserve Bank of India has been reporting the number of counterfeit notes detected in the banking channel. During the Second World War, Japanese operations to destabilise the Indian currency involved high quality forgeries, largely of Rupees Ten notes signed by Sir C.D. Deshmukh.[182] During 1945-46, a record 23,792 forged notes were detected as against 12,675 in the previous year.[183]

Recent Trends on Counterfeit Notes Detected

Together with the increase in number of notes in circulation, the number of counterfeit notes detected in the system has increased over the years. According to the Reserve Bank of India's data, while in 2000-01, 102,687 counterfeit notes were detected, in 2008-09, the number of counterfeit notes detected was 398,111. If these figures are compared with the total notes in circulation in the corresponding years, there were three counterfeit notes per million notes in circulation during 2000-01, which increased to eight counterfeit notes per million notes during 2008-09.[184]

An important case involving perhaps the largest single haul of counterfeit notes in a currency chest in the country was unearthed in 2008 in the state of Uttar Pradesh. In July of that year, the Special Task Force of the State police seized a large number of counterfeit notes from a person. Investigations revealed the involvement of a cashier of the currency chest of a nationalised bank branch in Dumariaganj, located 30 kms south of the border with Nepal. The police, along with a team of officials from the Reserve Bank of India and the concerned bank carried out a special scrutiny of the cash balances at the currency chest. In addition to shortage of balances in cash, more than 75,000 pieces of counterfeit notes were detected. Many of them were in the two higher denominations of Rs 500 and Rs 1,000. The face value of the counterfeit notes was to the tune of Rs 4.02 crore.[185]

This incident sent shock waves across the banking system as it was deemed to be a failure of the controls in the currency chest operations. The Reserve Bank was forced to take corrective action. A High Level Group headed by the then Deputy Governor, Usha Thorat was immediately constituted to review the existing arrangements for stocking and distribution of currency notes. The Group, in its report submitted a year later in August, 2009 recommended, inter-alia, measures for facilitating detection of counterfeit notes and maintaining quality of notes in circulation.

More recently, the number of counterfeit notes detected in 2015-16 had increased to 632,926. Still, as a proportion of the total notes in circulation during that year, their number was seven counterfeit notes per million notes in circulation.[186] During 2016-17, the year in which high value notes were demonetised, 762,072[187] counterfeit notes were detected. This is an all-time high so far.

Following the demonetisation, new design currency notes were issued in all denominations in a phased manner. As a result, the number of counterfeit notes detected in the banking channel showed a constant decline till 2020-21, when the number of counterfeit notes detected was 208,625[188], which was the lowest in 13 years.

However, during 2021-22 the counterfeit notes detected increased to 230,971. Of these, about 40 per cent were in the ₹100 denomination and about 34 per cent in the ₹500 denomination.[189]

Data on Fake Notes Seized

The National Crime Records Bureau, under the Ministry of Home Affairs, also reports details of Fake Indian Currency Notes (FICNs) which have been seized by law-enforcement agencies. During 2016-17, it designed a uniform proforma for collection of FICN data as well as web-enabled software for uploading the data on FICN by banks and law enforcement agencies.

According to its latest data, for the year 2021, police agencies seized 310,080 FICNs with value of over ₹20.39 crore. Of these, as many as 60,915 notes were of ₹2,000 denomination having face value of ₹12.18 crore.[190] Various other agencies, such as the Border Security Force, the Central Reserve Police Force and the Central Board of Indirect Taxes and Customs, also seized FICNs during the course of their operations. For instance, during 2021, the Central Board of Indirect Taxes and Customs seized FICNs with face value of ₹38.10 crore.[191]

Interestingly, the term Fake Indian Currency Note (FICN), which is also used for counterfeit notes, has its origin in a Customs notification of 2008. The Government, through its Notification No. 43/2008 - CUSTOMS (N.T.) dated May 13, 2008, specified "Fake Indian Currency Notes" as goods falling in the category of prohibited goods for the purposes of Section 135 of the Customs Act, 1962.[192]

Caveat on Data

All data regarding counterfeit notes need to be taken with a pinch of salt. The figure of counterfeit notes provided by Reserve Bank of India does not include counterfeit notes seized by police and other enforcement authorities. Moreover, all data on counterfeit notes pertains to notes detected or seized and not the actual number of such notes in the system. It can safely be said that the actual number of counterfeit notes circulating in the economy would be far higher than the figures mentioned above.

The stock of counterfeits at any point of time depends upon the quantum of counterfeit notes getting inducted into the system, as well as the length of time they circulate before being eliminated.[193] The more time the counterfeit notes remain in the system before being detected, the more would be the actual counterfeit notes per million notes in circulation in the economy.

At the global level, the Financial Action Task Force (FATF) report of 2013 found that the Indian rupee was the ninth most counterfeited currency in terms of its value and stood third in terms of the number of FICN detected around the world.[194]

A 2016 study on estimation of the quantum of FICN by the Indian Statistical Institute, Kolkata concluded that ₹400 crore of fake currency is in circulation in the country. Further, ₹70 crore of FICN are infused into the system every year, while agencies are able to intercept one-third of them. The study found that fake ₹1,000 notes formed about 50 per cent of the total value of fake notes.[195]

Consequences

Counterfeit notes in the economy leads to more money getting circulated in the system and can impact inflation. If counterfeits are large in number, the confidence in the acceptability of the country's currency may diminish. Fake notes are also used to fund terrorist activities. Injection of fake notes in a country's economy is a form of economic terrorism meant to manipulate its economy.

On November 8, 2016, in his speech announcing demonetisation of 500 and 1,000 rupee notes, the Prime Minister linked terrorist activities to fake currency notes. He said that enemies from across the border run their (terrorist) operations using fake currency notes. This has been going on for years. Many times, those using fake five hundred and thousand rupee notes have been caught and many such notes have been seized.[196]

As reported by various sources, most counterfeit Indian currency notes are printed in Pakistan and either moved directly into India or through a network of other countries. Major transit points include India's neighbours, Nepal and Bangladesh and Dubai. Nepal is extensively used by traffickers because of the porous borders it shares with India.[197]

Investigations by the National Investigation Agency and other agencies have established that FICNs have been used to fund terrorist/insurgent groups active in India. For instance, the Lashkar-e-Toiba operative David C. Headley, in his disclosures to US authorities, confessed to having been given FICNs of ₹250,000 in Pakistan by his handler for a trip to India to set up the plot for the 26/11 (November 26, 2008), Mumbai terrorist attacks.[198]

The Challenge and the Response

Counterfeiting is a constant challenge for issuers of currency, who have to be forever vigilant to remain ahead of counterfeiters. That is why the precise technical details of the materials used in making of currency notes are never shared publically. On the other hand, the users of currency – which means practically the entire population – need to be made aware of the features of currency notes so that they can distinguish a genuine note from a forged one. That is an existential dilemma that confronts the note issuing authorities.

Prior to 1861, when individual banks were issuing their currency notes, forgeries kept recurring from time to time. Most early notes were registered notes and the peer group within which these notes circulated was limited. This was the most effective deterrent against forgeries.[199] However, with the Government taking over the responsibility of note issue, over a period of time, the design and printing of notes became more sophisticated. Watermark and security thread were the most commonly used security features in early period notes.

Until 1956, it was the practice for notes of denomination of Rs 100 and above in circulation to be registered in the books of the Issue Department of the Reserve Bank of India. The registration sections in the Issue Offices maintained a record of all 'registered' notes issued and cancelled.[200] But with increasing number of notes in circulation, this practice had to be given up.

Moreover, with advancements in printing technology, many new security features were introduced in currency notes. These features are also periodically changed and upgraded with the objective of making counterfeiting difficult. For instance, the replacement of Ashoka Pillar series of notes with Mahatma Gandhi series in the late 1990s was initiated due to the difficulty in identifying counterfeits in the former series of notes by the public. The new series of notes had additional security features such as the windowed security thread, latent (hidden) denominational image, microprinting and raised identification mark as anti-counterfeiting measures.[201]

About seven years later, in 2004, the government approved incorporation of additional security features in Indian notes based on the suggestions of a high-level committee. These included an India-specific security feature called M-feature, a chemical to be incorporated at the paper-making stage and colour shift thread for notes of a Hundred rupees and higher denomination.[202]

Accordingly, in 2005-06, Reserve Bank of India introduced several new and additional features in notes. These included, demetallised, magnetic and machine readable windowed security thread with colour shift, improved intaglio printing, improved see-through feature having denominational numeral, and electrolyte watermark having denominational numeral alongside Mahatma Gandhi portrait in the watermark window.[203] These features were widely publicised through the banks. After demonetisation in 2016, the colour and design of notes in all denominations were again changed. However, since then, here have been no changes in the design or security features of notes.

Legal Provisions

Until 1899, there were no legal provisions for dealing with counterfeit notes as paper currency was still very new. In that year, Sections 489A, 489B, 489C, 489D were introduced in the Indian Penal Code, 1860 to protect currency notes from forgery. In 1943, Section 489E was added. At present, Sections 178, 179, 180, 181 and 182 of the Bharatiya Nyay Sanhita, 2023 constitute the legal framework for dealing with counterfeit notes.

These sections deal with counterfeiting of notes, using counterfeit notes as genuine notes, being in possession of counterfeit notes, making or possessing machinery or material for counterfeiting notes, and making or using documents resembling notes.

In all these sections, the words used are 'currency-notes' and 'bank-notes' while, for the sake of simplicity, we have used the word 'notes'. In these Sections, the expression 'bank-note' means any promissory note for the payment of money to bearer on demand, issued by any person carrying on the business of banking in any part of the world, or issued by or under the authority of any State or Sovereign Power, and intended to be used as money.

The specific Sections, type of offence and punishment prescribed are as follows:

- Section 178 deals with counterfeiting of notes. This is a cognizable and non-bailable offence, punishable with imprisonment for life or up to ten years and fine.
- Section 179 deals with using as genuine, forged or counterfeit notes, knowingly. This is a cognizable and non-bailable offence, punishable with imprisonment for life or up to ten years and fine.
- Section 180 deals with possession of forged or counterfeit notes. This is a cognizable and non-bailable offence, punishable with seven years of imprisonment or fine or both.
- Section 181 deals with making or possessing an instrument or material for forging or counterfeiting notes. This is a cognizable and non-bailable offence, punishable with imprisonment for life or up to ten years and fine.
- Section 182 deals with making or using documents resembling notes. This is a non-cognizable and bailable offence, punishable with fine up to six hundred rupees.

Courts have held in several cases that mere possession of counterfeit notes is not a crime. Further, even using counterfeit notes is not enough to make it an offence. The legal provisions are not meant to punish unwary possessors or users (of counterfeit notes). It has been held by courts that mens rea is essential for conviction of offences under Sections 489B and 489C of the Indian Penal Code.

Mens rea is the mental state or intention on the part of the accused to commit the offence. It is for the prosecution to prove that the accused, knowing that the note is counterfeit, intended to use it as genuine.

Interestingly, in a case (Umashanker v. State of Chhattisgarh[204]), involving using a fake currency note of Rs 100, the question of mens rea was examined by the Supreme Court of India. The case went as follows: On May 25, 1990 at about 10 pm, the appellant purchased one kilogram of mangoes costing Rs 5 by paying a fake currency-note of Rs 100. He was handed over to police who recovered 13 more such fake currency-notes from him. Charges were framed against him under Sections 489A, 489B and 489C of Indian Penal Code. In 1991, the Sessions Court, Bilaspur found him guilty of charges under Sections 489B and 489C and sentenced him to three years' rigorous imprisonment on each count. On appeal, in 1999, the High Court of Madhya Pradesh confirmed the conviction but reduced the sentence to two years' rigorous imprisonment under Section 489B and one year's rigorous imprisonment under Section 489C. When the case went in appeal to the Supreme Court of India, the Hon'ble Court, in its judgement in 2001, held that the mens rea of offences under these Sections is, "knowing or having reason to believe the currency-notes or bank notes to be forged or counterfeit". Without the afore-mentioned mens rea, a case under Sections 489B and 489C cannot be made. It observed that no material is brought on record by the prosecution to show that the appellant had the requisite mens rea. The Hon'ble Court set aside the conviction and sentence passed by the High Court and acquitted the appellant.

Another aspect considered by the courts when considering cases of counterfeit currency is to see whether at a casual glance, the currency note can be recognized as fake by a person of average intelligence.

Thus, in various courts of law, many cases of usage of counterfeit notes do not result in conviction in the absence of conclusive proof.

Another law that has been made applicable to counterfeiting of currency is the Unlawful Activities (Prevention) Act, 1967. In 2013, this law was amended by inserting Section 15 (iii a) in the Act, thereby bringing the damage to the monetary stability of India by way of production, smuggling or circulation of high-quality fake Indian paper currency, coin or any other material within the definition of a terrorist act. Sections 17 and 40 were also amended to provide that the punishment for raising funds for terrorist acts, and for offences for terrorist acts would include those through production, smuggling or circulation of high quality counterfeit Indian currency. Provisions of forfeiture of such currency were also included in Section 33.

Under the powers of the Act, the Government also framed the Investigation of High Quality Counterfeit Indian Currency Offences Rules, 2013. Section 5 of these Rules prescribes that the damage to monetary stability as mentioned in Section 15, shall be deemed to have been caused if the seizure of high quality counterfeit Indian currency is not less than Rupees One lakh, provided that the limit would not apply in case the currency has been intercepted at the international border, international airport or immigration check post.

These Rules also provide that the Bharatiya Reserve Bank Note Mudran Private Limited and the Security Printing and Minting Corporation of India Limited shall annually conduct a review of the counterfeit currency analysed by them during the period and submit a report to Reserve Bank of India for recommending to the Central Government, revisions to the Third Schedule of the Unlawful Activities (Prevention) Act, 1967.

At present, the Third Schedule of this Act defines the features of high quality counterfeit Indian currency notes as watermarks, security thread and any one of the following features: latent image, see-through registration, print quality sharpness, raised effect, fluorescent characteristics, substrate quality, paper taggant, colour shift effect in optically variable ink and colour shift effect in security thread. A counterfeit note having watermarks, security thread and any one of the above features would be classified as a high quality counterfeit note for the purpose of this Act.

Other measures have also been taken to deal with the problem of counterfeit notes. A FICN Coordination Group has been formed by the Ministry of Home Affairs to share intelligence and information amongst the different security agencies of the states/ centre to counter the problem of fake currency notes in the country. A 'Terror Funding and Fake Currency Cell' has been constituted in the National Investigation Agency to conduct focused investigation of terror funding and fake currency cases.[205]

Procedure for Dealing with Counterfeit Notes

Many times, when banks or members of public come into possession of a currency note that is known to be counterfeit, there is a tendency to destroy it as it carries no value. Moreover, they do not wish to get into procedural formalities of reporting the forgery to authorities. Many counterfeit notes meet this fate when detected. However, as far as banks are concerned, Reserve Bank of India has issued instructions, casting upon them responsibility in the matter.

Reserve Bank of India has authorised all banks, treasuries and sub-treasuries to impound any counterfeit note that comes to them. The value for a counterfeit note should not be given to the person tendering it. In no case, the counterfeit notes should be returned to the tenderer or destroyed by the bank branches/ treasuries. Failure to impound the counterfeit notes detected at their end would be construed as wilful involvement of the bank concerned in circulating counterfeit notes and penalty will be imposed.[206]

It has been provided that the bank branch has to put a stamp 'COUNTERFEIT NOTE' on the note and keep its record in a separate register. A receipt has to be issued to the person tendering the note.

Every bank is required to appoint a Nodal Bank Officer in each district to serve as the contact point for all counterfeit notes related activities. All reporting of counterfeit notes should be through the Nodal Bank Officer. At their Head Offices, banks are required to establish Forged Note Vigilance Cells to deal with matters relating to counterfeit notes.

Banks are required to report the details of counterfeit notes detected and impounded at their branches to police authorities, along with the impounded notes. A copy of the report has also to be sent to Reserve Bank of India and the bank's Head Office every month. However, if five or more pieces of counterfeit notes are detected in a single transaction, the counterfeit notes are to be forwarded immediately to the local police authorities for investigation by filing FIR (First Information Report), without waiting for the end of the month.

Banks have also been advised to re-align their cash management in such a manner so as to ensure that cash receipts in the denominations of ₹100 and above are not put into re-circulation without the notes being machine processed for authenticity.[207] This would ensure that all notes which are received in banks pass through note sorting machines before being put into circulation again. In case there are any counterfeits, these would be detected and prevented from going back into circulation.

But, getting these instructions implemented at branch level across the length and breadth of the country remains a challenge. As almost everyone who has been to a bank branch would have seen, most banks issue to the public as payments the very same notes that are received by them from the customers as receipts.

Similarly, it is highly doubtful if all counterfeit notes that are coming to the notice of banks are being reported. In 2013, the Reserve Bank of India had proposed a scheme providing for incentive to be given to banks for reporting of counterfeit notes[208] but it was withdrawn.

Increasing Awareness

It is in the interest of the economy that counterfeit notes are detected and reported to the maximum extent. For this, it is essential that both the public as well as staff members of banks are skilled to distinguish between genuine and counterfeit notes. For bankers, the Reserve Bank of India has instructed that banks and treasuries should ensure that the cash handling staff are fully conversant with the security features of a banknote. Further, banks should be equipped with ultra-violet lamps and banknote sorting/ detection machines to facilitate detection of counterfeit notes.[209] It also provides faculty support to banks and other interested institutions for training of their staff in detecting counterfeit notes.

To familiarise the public, the Reserve Bank of India has put into public domain the security features of currency notes on the link https://paisaboltahai.rbi.org.in on its website. It has also made available the design and security features of banknotes to the bank branches as posters for displaying the same prominently for members of the public.

The ₹2000 denomination banknotes in the **Mahatma Gandhi (New) Series** bear signature of the Governor, Reserve Bank of India. The note has motif of "Mangalyaan" on the reverse, depicting the country's first venture in the interplanetary space. The base colour of the note is magenta. The note has other designs and geometric patterns aligning with the overall colour scheme, both at obverse and reverse.

The size of the note is 66 mm x 166 mm

Features of the ₹2000 Note

Obverse:

1 See through register with denominational numeral 2000
2 Latent image with denominational numeral 2000
3 Denominational numeral २००० in Devnagari
4 Portrait of Mahatma Gandhi at the centre
5 Micro letters 'भारत' and 'India'.
6 Colour shift windowed security thread with inscriptions 'भारत', 'RBI' and '2000'. Colour of the thread changes from green to blue when the note is tilted
7 Guarantee Clause, Governor's signature with Promise Clause and RBI emblem towards right of Mahatma Gandhi's portrait
8 Mahatma Gandhi's portrait and electrotype (2000) watermarks
9 Number panel with numerals in ascending font on the top left side and bottom right side
10 Denominational numeral with Rupee Symbol, (₹2000) in colour changing ink (green to blue) on bottom right
11 Ashoka Pillar emblem on the right

Some features for visually impaired:

12 Intaglio or raised printing of Mahatma Gandhi portrait (4), Ashoka pillar emblem (11), horizontal rectangle identification mark with ₹2000 on the right, seven angular bleed lines both on the left and right sides

Reverse:

13 Year of printing of the note on the left
14 Swachh Bharat logo with slogan
15 Language panel
16 Motif of Mangalyaan
17 Denominational numeral २००० in Devnagari

Issued in public interest by

A Reserve Bank of India poster on security features of ₹2,000 notes

Endnote

Despite the extent of existence of counterfeit notes not being available, measures have been taken to check this menace. While security features of notes are updated periodically, legal as well as administrative framework has also been strengthened. The reporting mechanism needs to be more effective and the public awareness requires to be improved.

In the next part of our story, we will look at the phenomenon where notes are stripped of their legal status and become worthless pieces of paper in the hands of the holders. This phenomenon, called demonetisation, has taken place thrice in India so far, in 1946, 1978 and 2016. The last one was the most pervasive, when about 87 per cent of the value of currency in the country was demonetised.

Chapter Nine

Stripped of Value

When currency notes are stripped of their status as legal tender, it is called demonetisation. The demonetised currency notes no longer carry value and cannot be used for any transactions. Demonetisation has been used by many countries to overcome hyperinflation, curb black money, foster economic stability or to remove counterfeit currency. In India, demonetisation has been resorted to on three occasions so far: in 1946, 1978 and 2016. On the first two occasions, notes in the top three highest denominations were demonetised. The last occasion saw notes in the top two highest denominations being demonetised. While the earlier two occasions of demonetisation had limited impact, the last one affected practically the entire population. The objectives of the three demonetisations were broadly similar: to curb unaccounted money and illicit transactions. The success or otherwise of these moves has often been debated. The story of the three episodes of demonetisation is narrated in this chapter.

As we know, our banknotes carry on their face the words 'I promise to pay the bearer...' in capital letters. So the question naturally arises in our minds is how then can these notes be stripped of their value and what is the sanctity of the promise made thereon.

The answer to this question is that there is a provision for such a measure under the Reserve Bank of India Act, 1934. Section 26(2) of the Act provides that on recommendation of the Central Board (of the Reserve Bank of India), the Central Government may declare any series of bank notes of any denomination to cease to be legal tender. This can be done through a notification in the Gazette of India and would be effective from the date specified in the notification.

During the history of paper currency in India, there have been three instances so far when the legal status, conferred on certain denominations of currency notes, has been withdrawn, transforming them from precious valuable notes into mere pieces of printed paper. All three occasions have had much in common.

First, the element of surprise: the decisions to demonetise certain notes were announced all of a sudden, without any warning or prior notice. Second, those in possession of these notes were given limited time to exchange them. Third, the differences between the Reserve Bank of India and the Government of India have come out in the open while carrying out these moves. And fourth, the objectives with which demonetisation was carried out were not significantly achieved. In this part of our story, we look in some detail at each of the three instances of demonetisation that took place in 1946, 1978 and 2016.

The First Time: 1946

One consequence of the Second World War was widespread black marketing in daily items of consumption like food and cloth and tax evasion. It was felt that businessmen in India had amassed huge sums of wealth and evaded paying tax. In 1945, the Bank of England had withdrawn from circulation notes of ten pounds and above. Similar action was suggested for India to fight against black market money and tax evasion, which had assumed enormous proportions.

The Government consulted the Governor and Deputy Governor of Reserve Bank of India regarding demonetisation towards the end of 1945 but they were not enthusiastic about the scheme and expressed certain reservations.

However, the Government went ahead and issued two Ordinances on January 12, 1946. The first (ordinance) required all banks and Government treasuries in British India to furnish to the Reserve Bank of India by 3 pm on the same day, their holdings of bank notes of Rs 100, Rs 500, Rs 1,000 and Rs 10,000 as at the close of business on the previous day. The second (ordinance) demonetised bank notes of Rs 500 and above with effect from the expiry of January 12, 1946. Many Indian States also issued parallel Ordinances.[210] Initially, a limit of ten days was provided to exchange the notes; however the time limit was extended a number of times.

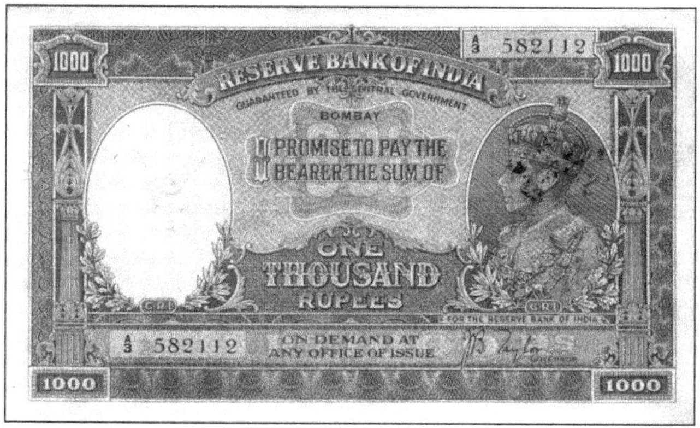

A 1,000 rupees denomination note demonetised in 1946[211]

The measure did not succeed, as by the end of 1947, out of a total issue of Rs. 143.97 crores of the high denomination notes, notes of the value of Rs. 134.9 crores were exchanged.[212] Thus, only about 6.3 per cent of the notes, which were not presented for exchange, could be said to have been demonetised.

Sir C. D. Deshmukh, who was Governor of Reserve Bank of India during that time, in a lecture in 1957, termed it as not a revolutionary measure and even its purpose as a minatory and punitive gesture towards black-marketing was not effectively served.[213]

As the higher denomination notes were not accessible to common people at that time, the currency ban did not have much impact on the common people and the Indian economy. The stock market rallied for two continuous years post the demonetisation reflecting impact on economic activity.[214]

Most reactions to the move were critical. Babu Rajendra Prasad, Member, Congress Working Committee, who subsequently became the first President of India, in an interview to the 'Daily Tej' said, "A large number of people belonging to the middle and lower-middle classes will be hit hard. Many of the war-time Ordinances succeeded in complicating the problems they were intended to solve in creating opportunities for corruption." Indeed, according to newspaper reports, a large number of Rs 500, Rs 1,000 and Rs 10,000 notes were exchanged unofficially at 60 to 70 per cent of their original value.[215]

Four years later, in 1950, the Rural Banking Enquiry Committee remarked on the need to provide adequate facilities for exchanging notes throughout the country. It was thought that high denomination notes would help reduce the physical quantity of notes in circulation. Accordingly, a bill to reissue high denomination notes was passed by Parliament in December 1953 amidst fear of members that they would encourage 'black-marketeers'.[216] All the three denominations were reintroduced in April 1954 with completely different design, watermark and colour scheme from the earlier notes.

The Second Instance: 1978

The year 1977 saw significant changes in government and the Reserve Bank of India. For the first time in independent India, the Congress Party lost the national election in March that year. A new Janata Party Government took over with Morarji Desai as Prime Minister. The year also saw three Governors of the Reserve Bank of India. In May, K.R. Puri stepped down and was replaced by M. Narasimham, who held office for just seven months. In December, Dr I.G. Patel was appointed Governor for a five-year term.

Just over a month later, the new Government, keen to display its 'social justice', issued an Ordinance to demonetise high value currency notes in denominations of Rs 1,000, 5,000 and 10,000 from January 17, 1978. As per the ordinance, the decision was taken in public interest as high denomination notes facilitated the illicit transfer of money for financing transactions harmful to the national economy. All banks and government treasuries were closed on that date and the public were given three days to surrender the notes for conversion.

Interestingly, on January 14, 1978, the government called a senior Reserve Bank of India official in the Chief Accountant's Office to come to Delhi for some urgent work. When he enquired about the purpose of the visit, he was told that matters related to exchange control would be discussed. On reaching Delhi, it was revealed that the government had decided to demonetize high denomination notes and he was required to draft the necessary Ordinance within twenty-four hours. During this period, no communication was allowed with the Bank's Central Office at Mumbai since such contacts could give rise to speculation. The draft Ordinance was completed on schedule; it was then finalized and sent for the signature of the President of India, Neelam Sanjiva Reddy in the early hours of January 16, 1978. The news was announced on All India Radio's news bulletin at 9 am the same day; it was given as a flash towards the end of the news bulletin.[217]

The decision was taken in utmost secrecy, with the Reserve Bank of India being involved just three days earlier.

Although Governor I.G. Patel went along with the move, he was unconvinced about its effectiveness. In his memoirs, he observed that the move was political in nature and that he was not in favour of the exercise. He recalled that when the Finance Minister informed him of the impending decision, he pointed out that 'such exercises seldom produce striking results' and that 'the idea that black money or wealth is held in the form of notes tucked away in suitcases or pillow cases is naive'.[218]

A 10,000 rupees denomination note demonetised in 1978[219]

At that time, demonetisation received limited public attention and had little impact on the daily lives of people. The notes demonetised formed just a minuscule fraction - about 0.6% - of the total currency in circulation. Further, the demonetised notes were of significantly high value, having little use for common people. A large portion - 45% of the high denomination notes in circulation or about 53% of the high denomination notes tendered for conversion - were with banks and government treasuries and not with the public.[220]

A cartoon on demonetisation of 1978 by R K Laxman

At the time of demonetisation, total value of high denomination notes in circulation was Rs 145.42 crores. Of this, Rs 124.45 crores of notes was tendered for conversion up to June, 1978 and Rs 116.31 crores passed for exchange in lower denominations.[221]

After the demonetisation, the one hundred rupee note remained the highest denomination currency note in the country for about a decade, till the five hundred rupee note was introduced in 1987. Thirteen years later, in 2000, the one thousand rupee note also made a comeback, for the second time.

And the Third Occasion: 2016

In 2014, the Congress-led Government at the centre was replaced by a Bharatiya Janata Party (BJP)-led Government. The BJP, on its own, got a comfortable majority in the lower house of Parliament. By the summer of 2016, Prime Minister Narendra Modi had completed two years in office. With a comfortable majority in the lower House of Parliament, the Government had the capacity to take bold decisions. The next general election was also nearly three years away. It was during those months that the scheme of demonetisation of high value notes was taking shape in the corridors of power.

The three-year term of Dr Raghuram Rajan, Governor, Reserve Bank of India was due to end in September. However, he was under attack from various quarters and there were reports that he might not get an extension. On June 18, 2016 in a surprise Sunday email to his staff, the Governor announced that "on due reflection, and after consultation with the government, I want to share with you that I will be returning to academia when my term as Governor ends on September 4, 2016."[222] That paved the way for appointment of a new Governor. Two weeks before Dr Rajan's term was to end, the name of the new Governor was announced. Dr Urjit Patel, who was serving as Deputy Governor, took over as Governor on September 5, 2016.

Just over two months later and a week after the festivities of the most important festival of India (Diwali) had ended, on November

8, 2016, in an evening address to the nation on radio and television, Prime Minister Narendra Modi announced the decision of the Government to render illegal the ₹500 and ₹1000 denomination notes from midnight. The hour-long address, in Hindi and English, took the nation by surprise. After giving a 15-minute background, the Prime Minister announced,

"Brothers and sisters,

To break the grip of corruption and black money, we have decided that the five hundred rupee and thousand rupee currency notes presently in use will no longer be legal tender from midnight tonight that is 8th November 2016. This means that these notes will not be acceptable for transactions from midnight onwards. The five hundred and thousand rupee notes hoarded by anti-national and anti-social elements will become just worthless pieces of paper. The rights and the interests of honest, hard-working people will be fully protected. Let me assure you that notes of one hundred, fifty, twenty, ten, five, two and one rupee and all coins will remain legal tender and will not be affected."[223]

Further on, in his speech he gave the objectives which this measure sought to achieve and sought the support of the people,

"In this fight against corruption, black money, fake notes and terrorism, in this movement for purifying our country, will our people not put up with difficulties for some days? ... In a country's history, there come moments when every person feels he too should be part of that moment; that he too should make his contribution to the country's progress. Such moments come but rarely. Now, we again have an opportunity where every citizen can join this mahayajna against the ills of corruption, black money and fake notes. The more help you give in this campaign, the more successful it will be."[224]

On the date of demonetisation, the total currency in circulation was ₹17.7 lakh crore (trillion), of which ₹500 and ₹1,000 denominations accounted for ₹15.44 lakh crore (trillion).[225] Thus, these two highest denomination notes formed about 87 per cent of the total value of notes in circulation at that time. This was in stark contrast to the earlier rounds of demonetisation, when the demonetised currency formed a miniscule part of the total currency. Therefore, the magnitude and impact of this demonetisation was bound to be massive.

Interestingly, the ₹1,000 currency note has been unlucky in the sense that it has had to bear the brunt of demonetisation on all the three occasions. After the formation of the Reserve Bank of India, the note was first introduced in 1938 and had a life span of just eight years before it was demonetised in 1946. It was re-introduced eight years later in 1954 but demonetised once again in 1978. It was again introduced in 2000, only to be demonetised for the third time in 2016. Since then, the note has not been issued so far.

Following the announcement, the Reserve Bank of India declared all banks in the country closed on the following day (November 9, 2016) and formulated a scheme for exchange/ deposit of the higher denomination notes, technically called Specified Bank Notes (or SBNs). Under it, members of public were advised to deposit SBNs till December 30, 2016 in their bank account or exchange these for other legal tender notes up to specified limits across the country. The exchange of SBNs was allowed at district central co-operative banks from November 10-14, 2016 and at commercial bank branches till November 25, 2016. Subsequently, the exchange facility was restricted to the Reserve Bank of India Offices[226] but the deposit facility continued till December 30, 2016.

Interestingly, during this spell of demonetisation, neither the Government of India nor the Reserve Bank of India used the word 'demonetisation' in their notifications. The term Specified Bank Notes (SBNs) was coined to refer to the demonetised notes and these notes ceased to be legal tender, as per the notifications. Further, while on the earlier two demonetisation occasions, the government had issued an ordinance to give effect to the measure, in 2016, the act was carried out through a notification in the Gazette of India.

Initially, limits on withdrawal from bank counters and ATMs were imposed to gradually meet the demand for new currency following the demonetisation. However, these limits were modified and relaxed several times in line with the evolving situation leading to considerable confusion among the people. Reserve Bank of India issued as many as 57 official circulars between November 9 and December 31, 2016 revising the conditions under which the public could make deposits, withdrawals, and exchanges of the demonetised currency.[227]

A ₹500 denomination note demonetised in 2016

Unlike the previous instances of demonetisation, the demonetisation of 2016 affected the entire population of the country. Huge lines were witnessed outside bank branches and ATMs ran perpetually short of cash. The restrictions imposed on depositing and withdrawing money and the frequent changes in rules complicated matters further. Particularly in the initial weeks, people faced enormous difficulties in getting their notes exchanged.

The opposition parties were quick to play up the resentment of the public to criticise the decision. In a short but powerful speech in the parliament, Dr Manmohan Singh, former Prime Minister called the demonetisation exercise a 'case of organised loot, legalised plunder of the common people' and called the process 'monumental mismanagement' by the government.[228] Former Finance Minister P. Chidambaram called it a thoughtless move and a punishment to the poor. Several writ petitions were filed in various courts in the country challenging the decision of the Government to demonetise the higher denomination notes.

It was reported in the Press that like the previous occasions of demonetisation undertaken in the country, this time too, the Reserve Bank of India was not convinced about its outcome. In its Central Board meeting held about two and a half hours before the announcement of the decision, the Reserve Bank of India had warned that banning high-value cash was unlikely to have any substantial impact on tackling the black money menace. According to minutes of the meeting revealed by the RBI in an RTI reply, the central bank had red flagged concerns over the government claims on curbing black money and counterfeit notes, citing that most cash was in the form of real sector assets.[229]

A year after demonetisation, former Reserve Bank of India Governor Raghuram Rajan, in the introduction to his book 'I Do What I Do', stated that in February 2016, he was asked by the government for his views on demonetisation. In his views, given orally, he had indicated that although there might be long term benefits, he felt that the likely short-term economic costs would outweigh them and that there were potentially better alternatives to achieve the main goals. The Reserve Bank of India had prepared a note on the subject and given to the government. He further stated that 'at no point during my term was the RBI asked to make a decision on demonetisation'.[230]

The Supreme Court of India clubbed all the petitions against demonetisation in various courts and a five-member constitution bench heard the matter in late 2022. During the submissions made in the case, Reserve Bank of India mentioned that it had recommended demonetisation of higher denomination notes to the Government of India on November 8, 2016 in response to the Government's letter dated November 7, 2016. In its judgement of January 2, 2023, the Supreme Court of India upheld the decision of the Government by a 4-1 verdict.

Consequence

As most of the currency had gone out of circulation as a consequence of demonetisation, there was a need to remonetise the economy quickly. The introduction of ₹2,000 note was the first step towards quick remonetisation.[231] The Reserve Bank of India and the printing presses made concerted efforts to augment the production and supply of bank notes. Printing presses worked round the clock and air-lifting of notes was resorted to wherever required. As a result, the total notes in circulation increased rapidly to ₹15.06 trillion as on June 30, 2017, which was about 85 per cent of the notes in circulation on November 4, 2016.[232] Nearly one year after demonetisation, as on October 27, 2017, currency in circulation stood at 91 per cent of its pre-demonetisation level.[233]

An economic consequence of demonetisation was the increase in expenditure on printing of currency notes, which more than doubled due to requirement of larger volume of notes for replacement of the demonetised currency. The total expenditure incurred on security printing jumped from ₹34.2 billion in 2015-16 (July to June) to ₹79.65 billion in 2016-17 (July to June).[234]

The demonetised notes received were subjected to verification and counting in sophisticated high speed Currency Verification and Processing Systems in the Reserve Bank of India over a period of several months. The processing capacity had to be augmented by working night shifts and six days in a week. A year later, in its Annual Report for the year 2017-18, Reserve Bank of India reported that Specified Bank Notes of ₹15,310.73 billion had been returned from circulation.[235] It meant that 99.2 per cent of the demonetised currency notes had been exchanged back.

Outcome

The initial objectives of demonetisation were to attack black money, fake notes and terrorism. Subsequently, the digitisation of the economy also was brought into the discourse.

Initially, it was believed that the black money would not come back into the system as a result of demonetisation and it would become 'worthless pieces of paper'. But initial figures in the first two months made it clear that it was not to be. The final figures from the Reserve Bank of India punctured this belief. Critics were quick to point out that the main objective of demonetisation that it would unearth black money had been defeated as the entire money had been accounted for.

A year later, the government touted the following benefits of demonetisation in its Annual Report of the Ministry of Finance: elimination of fake currency and strike against terrorist activities; action against generation of black money; formalisation of economy and digitisation.[236] Elaborating, it mentioned that terrorist financing had stopped almost entirely; based on deposit of demonetised notes in bank accounts, 1,00,000 high risk cases for enforcement actions had been identified; informal money was brought into the banking and formal system leading to increased liquidity in the economy; and there was substantial progress in digital transactions, both in volume and value terms.

A 2017 paper commented that demonetisation involved criticism from all quarters and major inconvenience to the public at large.

There was a considerable drop in economic activity by about 1 per cent in Gross Domestic Product immediately after it and on account of currency squeeze even during remonetisation period there was an impact on several sectors of the economy albeit for a brief duration. The paper concluded that 'overall, the effects of demonetisation on the economy can be said to be neutral. Initially the economy suffered hiccups and the informal sector was largely affected. But the positive effects of demonetisation far outweigh the negative outcomes'.[237]

A cartoon on demonetisation of 2016 by Paresh Nath

One of the objectives of demonetisation was to attack the fake currency notes circulating in the system. During 2016-17, 762,072 pieces of counterfeit notes were detected in the banking system, 20.4 per cent higher than in the previous year. The Reserve Bank of India launched an exercise to estimate the density of fake currency notes during the counting and verification of demonetised notes. It was found that there was a significant pick-up in the rate of detection of fake currency notes at the Reserve Bank of India level in the post demonetisation period as compared to a year ago.[238] Since then, till 2021, the number of counterfeit notes detected in the banking system had been lower.

Soon after demonetisation, there was an increase in volume of digital transactions compared to traditional (cash) transactions, obviously due to the shortage of cash in the economy. However, a 2020 paper concluded that these patterns reversed somewhat in the coming months so that the traditional transactions volume returned to its pre-demonetisation level. The volume of digital transactions did fall back somewhat but stayed well above its pre-demonetisation level. The paper found that the value of digital transactions have been larger and have also been growing faster than traditional transactions for the past decade. However, demonetisation does not appear to have affected the trends or levels of either digital or traditional transactions.[239]

Another study, conducted two years after demonetisation, concluded that it had significant positive impact on tax base and tax collections, encouraged people to embrace digital methods, reduced cash flow to terror organisations and led to the dismantling of the counterfeit currency infrastructure. However, it came at a huge social and economic cost and caused great misery to the lives of common people.[240]

Five years after demonetisation, a former Economic Affairs and Finance Secretary to the Government of India commented that whether the (demonetised notes were) not hoarded as black money or the hoarders took advantage of legal and administrative loopholes in the demonetisation implementation mechanism to change the colour of money from black to white, the fact was that the entire demonetised currency came back to Reserve Bank of India. Weighing the pros and cons of the exercise, he stated that forced formalisation of India's large tax-evading informal economy was worth the short-term pain it caused in terms of loss of businesses and employment. But its impact on the elimination of corruption and black money has hardly been noticeable. It did have a good impact, at least initially, on curbing terrorist activities and the injection of counterfeit money. On account of the sheer nature of the operation, its implementation was chaotic and caused considerable pain. Nonetheless, it was completed in a fairly short period of time.[241]

The currency in circulation to GDP ratio, which was 12.1 per cent in March, 2016 (before demonetisation) fell to 8.7 per cent a year later (after demonetisation) but had bounced back to 12 per cent in March, 2020. In March, 2022 it was higher than the pre-demonetisation levels at 13.7 per cent[242], showing increased dominance of cash in the economy since demonetisation.

Endnote

Over five years after demonetisation, cash is back as king in the Indian economy despite the growth in digital payments. There is no data on reduction in black money and illegal cash deposited in bank accounts as a result of demonetisation. The inconvenience that the public faced has largely been forgotten. The economy has moved on with increased formalisation and the story of another demonetisation consigned to pages of history.

We are now approaching the end of our story. Paper currency has ruled supreme for two hundred years but is now threatened by technological developments, just like other spheres of our lives. Change is inevitable and the signs are already there. We will look at the alternatives to paper currency that have challenged its supremacy. In particular, we would touch upon polymer notes, plastic money, e-wallets, crypto-currency and, finally, the Central Bank Digital Currency.

Chapter Ten

Beyond Paper

Technological changes have swept the world, transforming all spheres of our lives. Currency notes have not remained immune to this change. After reigning supreme for nearly two centuries, paper currency notes found new rivals. These came in the form of polymer notes, plastic money in the form of credit and debit cards and a multitude of electronic wallets issued by both banks and non-banks. Still, the usage of cash continued its dominance. The last decade has seen the emergence of cryptocurrencies. Their increasing presence has forced central banks all over the world to think on developing their own digital currencies. India has already announced pilot projects towards the launch of a digital rupee. This has the potential to change the narrative for paper currency in the years ahead.

Innovation and technology has been the hallmark of human civilization. The evolution of money from barter and the evolution of paper money from metallic currencies were important turning points in the development of monetary systems. With increasing sophistication in technology, the focus remained on building newer and better security features into the paper currency notes. Paper had ruled supreme as material for currency notes till recent decades when a few countries upturned the stakes for paper and began switching to polymer notes.

Polymer Notes

The limited life of paper notes and increasing costs of printing led to the search for alternative materials for currency. The answer was found in polymer. Several countries started adopting polymer notes, starting with Australia in 1988. By 1996, Australia had completely switched to polymer currency. By now, over twenty countries including Canada, New Zealand, Vietnam, Thailand and the United Kingdom have fully or partially switched over to polymer notes and many more are in the process of doing so.

Although polymer notes - which are made from a thin sheet of polypropylene plastic sheet - are more expensive to produce as compared to paper notes, they have a 2.5 to 4x longer life-span. Moreover, these notes weigh less, are waterproof, crumple-free, difficult to tear, hard to counterfeit and fully recyclable. However, these are relatively difficult to fold and have a risk of fading. Still, many believe that the future of currency is polymer notes. So, paper currency can be said to have a competitor in polymer notes. As mentioned in an earlier chapter, India has not gone in for polymer notes despite considering the same for several years for reasons which have not been disclosed as yet.

Plastic Money

However, other challenges to the existence of paper currency have been more fundamental, threatening the very basics of currency. The first challenge to usage of currency notes itself came with the introduction of credit and debit cards which were commonly referred to as plastic money. Internationally, the first credit card, as we know it today, was the Diner's Club which appeared in the United States of America in 1949. But it was ten years later, in 1959, when American Express made the first plastic credit card. In 1969, the magnetic strip was invented and began being affixed at the back of credit cards. Debit cards were first introduced in 1966 and became popular with the spread of Automated Teller Machines (ATMs).

In India, though Citibank had introduced the Diner's Card in 1969, credit cards became popular after their introduction by two public sector banks, Andhra Bank and Central Bank of India, in the early 1980s. By the end of the decade, many other banks had also introduced such cards. Some of the banks allowed their cards to be used for withdrawal of cash from their branches or ATMs; these cards were the early debit cards.

During the next few years, these cards gained popularity and spread widely. Some people considered them as status symbols and possessed multiple cards of different banks. By January 2012, there were 177 lakh credit cards issued by 28 banks and 2680 lakh debit cards issued by 52 banks, outstanding in the country.[243]

During the initial years of introduction of credit and debit cards, some analysts felt that these would herald the end of cash. Plastic money was touted as the new form of money, which could displace currency notes. However, despite the increasing popularity and usage of credit and debit cards, there was no decline in the usage of hard cash.

The number of credit and debit cards has continued to increase over the years. The use of debit cards was widely popularised as the government introduced the Direct Benefit Transfer scheme in 2013 for crediting various government subsidies directly in the bank accounts of beneficiaries. Card usage also got a boost during the period following demonetisation in 2016 and the lockdowns during the Covid pandemic three years later.

In March 2022, the number of credit cards and debit cards had risen to 736 lakh and 9177 lakh respectively.[244] The value of payment transactions on credit and debit cards (at point of sale terminals and online) during 2021-22 was ₹9.72 and ₹7.30 lakh crore respectively.[245]

E-wallets or Prepaid Payment Instruments (PPIs)

Prepaid Payment Instruments (PPIs) are defined by the Reserve Bank of India as instruments that facilitate purchase of goods and services, financial services, remittance facilities, etc., against the value stored therein.[246] The most well known PPIs are commonly referred to as e-wallets, short for electronic wallets. An e-wallet is a type of electronic card which is linked to a user's bank account and used for transactions made online through a computer or smartphone. Just like a physical wallet, a user can store money in an e-wallet for any future online transaction. Thus, like debit or credit cards, it obviates the need for carrying physical paper currency notes in your physical wallet.

Oxigen Wallet is considered to be the first e-wallet in India, having been launched in July 2004. It was followed by Wallet365.com in 2006. Both these wallets failed to gain much popularity. In 2009, Mobikwik was launched, which marked the onset of digital transactions in India. Later, Paytm, Googlepay, Amazon Pay and Airtel Money made their entry. Banks have also launched their own e-wallets such as State Bank Buddy, ICICI Pockets and HDFC PayZapp.

There are various types of e-wallets that serve different purposes depending on the nature of the business and the end-users. Earlier, these were classified as closed, semi-closed or open wallets.

A closed wallet is issued by an entity for facilitating the purchase of goods or services from that entity only and does not permit cash withdrawal. Users of such wallets can only use the stored funds to complete a transaction only with the wallet's issuer. If a transaction is cancelled or a refund is issued, the entire amount is stored in the wallet. A semi-closed wallet allows users to make transactions only with listed merchants and at specific locations. Such wallets also do not permit cash withdrawal.

Open wallets are those provided by banks or institutions partnering with banks. Users with open wallets can use them for any type of transaction, including withdrawal of funds from banks and ATMs as well as transfer of funds. Payments can be made both online and in-store at any time. The transactions can be made from anywhere in the world; however, both the sender and the receiver must have accounts on the same application.

The above classification has since been modified. While there is no change in the definition of closed wallet, the other two types of wallets have now been classified by the Reserve Bank of India as Small PPIs and Full-KYC PPIs. Both these require prior approval/ authorisation from Reserve Bank of India before issuance. Small PPIs can only be used for purchase of goods and services at clearly identified merchant locations/ establishments which have a specific contract with the issuer and not for funds transfer or cash withdrawal. Full-KYC PPIs are issued by banks and non-banks after completing KYC (Know Your Customer) of the holder. Besides payments for goods and services, these can be used for funds transfer and cash withdrawal.[247]

The Reserve Bank of India has granted permission to about three dozen private entities (non-banks) to issue PPIs in the country. It has also framed rules and regulations which govern various aspects of such instruments under the Payment and Settlement Systems Act, 2007.

Transactions through PPIs started picking up from 2014-15; during that year 314 million (3,140 lakh) transactions valued at ₹212 billion (₹21,200 crore) were recorded.[248] Since then, there has been no looking back. During 2021-22, 65,812 lakh transactions valued at ₹2.94 lakh crore were reported.[249] The total number of PPI transactions in the country in March 2022 was 27,408 lakh[250] (2.7 billion), a phenomenal figure, indeed.

The new forms of money that have come up have been becoming increasingly popular over the years. A large number of transactions are now taking place through these modes, be it credit or debit cards or e-wallets. The average decadal growth rate of currency in circulation has declined from 15.1 to 12.6 between the decades 2001-10 and 2011-20, reflecting innovations in digital payments technology.[251] Two important events in the latter half of the last decade – the demonetisation of higher denomination notes in 2016 and the Covid pandemic in 2019-20 – must have contributed to this decline.

The ratio of CIC (currency in circulation) to Gross Domestic Product declined from 11.9 during 2001-10 to 11.3 during 2011-20.[252] However, this ratio was 14.4 and 13.7 during the years 2020-21 and 2021-22.[253] The decline of GDP (denominator in the above ratio) as a result of the Covid pandemic contributed considerably to the increase in the ratio during 2020-21.[254] Thus, despite all new forms of money that have become prevalent in recent years and their growing usage, the usage of paper money has remained paramount. But whether it will be able to maintain that position in the coming years, only Time would tell.

Cryptocurrencies

Cryptocurrencies are innovative virtual payments systems that do not rely on a central authority to generate currency supply, or to verify, record and track transactions. These currencies are characterised by being decentralized systems, where transactions are authenticated by participants themselves by consensus. These are anonymous, in the sense, that while the transactions are verified but not the purposes or their counterparties of transactions. Further, these are borderless, that is, they work over the internet without any physical existence or national borders.

They can, therefore, bypass the traditional financial system and all its controls. They can also not be traced or confiscated or frozen by Governments. As of May 2021, there were about 1,700 cryptocurrencies with a market capitalisation of at least $1 million each, and another

500 with a market capitalisation in excess of $100,000.[255] Bitcoin is, of course, the most dominant and well known.

Bitcoin is regarded as the first cryptocurrency. It was created in 2008 by an individual or a group of people going by the name of Satoshi Nakamoto, whose real identity has not been revealed till now. The launch was a low-key virtual event through an online paper, posted weeks after the Lehman Brothers went bankrupt, which set off the financial crisis in United States that affected financial institutions across the world. Bitcoin was intended as a medium of exchange that would facilitate execution of financial transactions outside the ambit of traditional institutions and government control, relying only on the digital identities of the transacting parties.

In the traditional financial system, transactions can be reversed or meddled with by third parties, and transaction costs can add up. Bitcoin was presented as a way to transact without using a third party. Rather, the Bitcoin system uses cryptographic proof to maintain the integrity of the network instead of relying on third-party banks and other institutions.

The technology adopted by Bitcoin is known as blockchain technology. Simply put, it is a form of storing information that prevents anyone from changing, hacking or cheating it. It is used to record transactions and track assets within a network of businesses. It stores transactional records (known as blocks) of the public in several databases (known as chain) in a network connected through peer to peer nodes. Typically, this storage is referred to as a digital ledger. The technology is also referred to as digital ledger technology.

In the early days, the first transactions with Bitcoin were negotiated on internet forums with people bartering for goods and services in exchange for Bitcoin. The value of Bitcoin was originally arbitrary. Once Bitcoin became available on exchanges in 2010, it became easier to buy, sell, trade and store. In February 2011, Bitcoin's price crossed the $1 threshold.

Interestingly, it took more than a year for the first economic transaction to take place, using Bitcoin. On May 18, 2010, a Floridian programmer named Laszlo Hanyecz posted on Bitcointalk.org forum that he was ready to pay 10,000 Bitcoin to buy pizza, preferably two large pies. Four days later, on May 22, his offer was accepted by a 19-year old who purchased two Papa John's pizzas, valued at $41, and delivered them to him for 10,000 Bitcoin. This was the first-ever recorded real-world transaction using cryptocurrency. It established the initial real-world value of Bitcoin at about 244 Bitcoins per dollar.

Nine months later, Bitcoin was valued at par with the dollar. Twelve years later, on May 22, 2022, one Bitcoin was valued at $29,491.51. Had Hanyecz decided to hold on to the 10,000 Bitcoin, they would have been worth $295 million on the twelfth anniversary of his purchase! In remembrance of that day, cryptocurrency fans and supporters still call May 22 as Pizza Day and celebrate by buying two pizzas and sharing them.

Following Bitcoin, several other cryptocurrencies came up, among them were Dogecoin (2013), Tether (2014), Ethereum (2015) and The Sandbox (2020).

For a medium of exchange to be reliable, it should have a reasonably stable value compared with the unit of account in which goods and services in an economy are priced. But this has not been true for Bitcoin, whose prices have fluctuated widely over the years. For instance, on Christmas Day in 2015, one Bitcoin was trading at $419; about two years later, on December 15, 2017, the value was $19,650, a forty-seven fold increase in two years. The value had come down to $15,075 on Christmas Day that year, a drop by around a quarter in just ten days.[256] At the end of December, 2024, a Bitcoin was trading at $103,645.

The price volatility is not unique to Bitcoin; the other cryptocurrencies also have the same characteristic. Ethereum, another popular cryptocurrency was trading at $8 on January 1, 2017 and shot up to $1,433 on January 12, 2018, a 179-fold increase. Within three months it fell to $385 and again surged to $812 a month later. In late May 2021, a unit of Ethereum was worth about $2,500.[257] As at the end of December, 2024, a unit of Ethereum was trading at $3,826.

Despite its volatility, Bitcoin has been officially adopted as legal tender in El Salvador alongside the dollar since September 2021 and in the Central African Republic since April, 2022. Several countries, including United States, Canada, France, Germany, Spain and Japan allow transactions in Bitcoin.

However, the Reserve Bank of India as well as the Government of India has taken a cautious approach to cryptocurrencies. In 2013, the Reserve Bank of India issued a Press Release cautioning the users of virtual currencies including Bitcoins about the potential financial, operational, legal, and other risks that they were exposing themselves to. It clarified that such currencies were not authorised by any central bank or monetary authority.[258]

In 2017, it reiterated that anyone dealing in virtual currencies would be doing so at their own risk. In April, 2018 Reserve Bank of India prohibited all banks, Non Banking Financial Companies and payment system providers from dealing in virtual currencies. This order was challenged in court and in March, 2020, the Supreme Court of India struck down the same as unconstitutional.

Since then, cryptocurrencies have become an important avenue for investors seeking quick and high returns, especially among the younger investors. Based on multiple studies, it is estimated that in 2021, over 100 million people in India owned cryptocurrencies. According to WazirX, the largest crypto exchange in the country, 70 per cent of its users are under thirty years of age.[259] There are about fifteen exchange platforms for trading and selling cryptocurrencies. India is believed to have the highest number of crypto owners in the world. Despite the proliferation of cryptocurrencies, the central bank of the country has continued with its tough stance towards them.

In a speech in 2022, the Deputy Governor of Reserve Bank of India made a scathing attack on cryptocurrencies and concluded, "We have seen that crypto-technology is underpinned by a philosophy to evade Government controls. Cryptocurrencies have specifically been developed to bypass the regulated financial system. These should be reason enough to treat them with caution. We have also seen that cryptocurrencies are not amenable to definition as a currency, asset or commodity; they have no underlying cash flows, they have no intrinsic value; that they are akin to Ponzi Schemes, and may even be worse. These should be reason enough to keep them away from the formal financial system. Additionally, they undermine financial integrity, especially the KYC regime and AML/CFT regulations and at least potentially facilitate anti-social activities. More substantially, they can (and if allowed most likely will) wreck the currency system, the monetary authority, the banking system, and in general Government's ability to control the economy. They threaten the financial sovereignty of a country and make it susceptible to strategic manipulation by private corporates creating these currencies or Governments that control them. All these factors lead to the conclusion that banning cryptocurrency is perhaps the most advisable choice open to India. We have examined the arguments proffered by those advocating that cryptocurrencies should be regulated and found that none of them stand up to basic scrutiny."[260]

As matters stand, cryptocurrencies continue to thrive in India as these are neither banned nor regulated. The government is planning to bring legislation for regulating cryptocurrencies, with the Cryptocurrency and Regulation of Official Digital Currency Bill, 2021 still in the framing stage. Since April, 2022, a 30 per cent tax has been imposed on income from transfer of any digital assets (which includes cryptocurrencies) as provided in the Union Budget for 2022-23. Since July, 2022, a tax deduction at source (TDS) of 1 per cent has also been fixed for transactions involving cryptocurrency.

Central Bank Digital Currency (CBDC)

As the concept of a Central Bank Digital Currency (CBDC) is still evolving, there is no universally accepted definition of a CBDC. A definition provided by International Monetary Fund staffers in their paper described CBDC as a digital representation of a sovereign currency issued by and as a liability of a jurisdiction's central bank or other monetary authority.[261] The Reserve Bank of India defines CBDC as the legal tender issued by a central bank in digital form.[262]

Basically, CBDC may be either retail or wholesale. Retail CBDC refers to the money we carry in our wallets (or e-wallets). Wholesale CBDC is the money used in settling inter-bank transactions or deployment of central bank reserves. In our story, we are referring to the retail CBDC while dealing with the subject. While retail CBDC may apparently appear to be similar to the electronic money we keep in our bank accounts and spend on our smartphones, a key difference is the absence of a commercial bank intermediary.

Retail CBDC can be issued directly by the central bank to the public. This form of issuance is called direct issuance. It can also be issued to intermediaries such as banks, who then issue it to the public, much like a fiat currency. This form of issuance is called indirect issuance.

Issuing of a CBDC is a complex national project that will involve multiple stakeholders beyond the traditional central bank counterparts such as ministry of Finance. Its impact would extend to the existing legal framework and may require changes in the governing, accounting and financial reporting standards. It will also affect agencies such as financial intelligence units, tax, capital market and statistical agencies. It would also require an adequately developed technological infrastructure.[263]

A CBDC has a variety of advantages over cash. The anonymity and non-traceability of cash transactions makes it a favoured medium of exchange for criminals and corrupt activities; usage of CBDC would put a check on such transactions. Replacing cash with CBDC would also discourage shadow economic transactions, which do not get reported resulting in siphoning off tax and government revenues. The vulnerability of paper currency to counterfeiting is also obviated in this form of currency. Printing paper currency incurs huge and ever rising costs; these costs can be avoided in CBDC. Besides all these, central banks would be at an advantage in monitoring monetary policy decisions in a CBDC environment.

However, there are downsides too. Some argue that the poor and unbanked households use cash as their main method of payment; they would be at a disadvantage if cash is eliminated. Cash also does not require electricity and technology in its usage; in case of disruption in technology or a natural disaster, cash may be the only way to transact. However, the major concern of CBDC stems from the loss of privacy in transactions and the fear that the state could monitor all your transactions, threatening free speech, assembly and dissent.

Another downside of CBDCs is that these may be subjected to cyber hacks and cyber threats. CBDCs could also impact the monetary policy of the country, which could lead to financial instability.

In the light of the above issues (as well as several others) relating to issuance of CBDC, many central banks are still considering the pros and cons of issuing retail CBDC. Only a very few have conducted limited-scale pilot issuance. In April, 2020 China became the first major economy to pilot digital currency.[264] A 2021 Bank for International Settlements (BIS) survey of central banks found that 86 per cent were actively researching the potential for CBDCs, 60 per cent were experimenting with the technology and 14 per cent were deploying pilot projects.[265]

Digital Rupee

India's Finance Minister Smt. Nirmala Sitharaman announced in the Union Budget for 2022-23 the issuance of a central bank-backed digital currency. During the course of her speech, she stated, "Introduction of Central Bank Digital Currency (CBDC) will give a big boost to digital economy. Digital currency will also lead to a more efficient and cheaper currency management system. It is, therefore, proposed to introduce Digital Rupee, using blockchain and other technologies, to be issued by the Reserve Bank of India starting 2022-23."[266]

In order to create awareness about the CBDCs in general and the planned features of the Digital Rupee (e₹), the Reserve Bank of India released a Concept Note on CBDC in October, 2022. The Note seeks to explain the approach of the Reserve Bank of India towards introduction of CBDC.[267] The concluding chapter of the Concept Note is given in Appendix V.

The Reserve Bank of India has already commenced work towards launching the Digital Rupee. In its Annual Report for 2021-22, it has stated that the design of CBDC needs to be in conformity with the stated objectives of monetary policy, financial stability and efficient operations of currency and payment systems. The Bank proposes to adopt a graded approach to introduction of CBDC, going step by step through stages of Proof of Concept, pilots and the launch.[268] The Bank is working towards a phased implementation of CBDC in both wholesale and retail segments.[269]

In November 2022, it announced commencement of pilot runs of the digital rupee for wholesale transactions. The beginning was made with nine banks (State Bank of India, Bank of Baroda, Union Bank of India, HDFC Bank, ICICI Bank, Kotak Mahindra Bank, Yes Bank, IDFC First Bank and HSBC) using the virtual currency for settlement of secondary market transactions in government securities.[270]

A month later, in December 2022, the pilot for the retail segment was launched in a closed user group comprising select customers and merchants. In this segment, the pilot would be executed in two phases. In the first phase, four banks (State Bank of India, ICICI Bank, Yes Bank and IDFC First Bank) will carry out the implementation in four cities, namely, Mumbai, New Delhi, Bengaluru and Bhubaneswar. In the second phase, four more banks (Bank of Baroda, Union Bank of India, HDFC Bank and Kotak Mahindra Bank) will join the pilot, which would be extended to nine other cities, namely, Ahmedabad, Gangtok, Guwahati, Hyderabad, Indore, Kochi, Lucknow, Patna and Shimla. The scope of the pilot may be expanded gradually to include more banks, users and locations.

The retail digital rupee will be issued in the same denominations that paper currency and coins are currently issued and distributed through banks. Transactions could be both person-to-person as well as person-to-merchant. It will offer features of physical cash like trust, safety and settlement finality. As in the case of cash, it will not earn any interest and can be converted to other forms of money like deposits with banks.[271]

However, there would be a lot of other work required to be done before a CBDC can be launched, even if the Reserve Bank of India is ready with its contours. For starters, a number of laws, such as Reserve Bank of India Act, 1934, the Coinage Act, 2011 the Foreign Exchange Management Act, 1999 and the Information Technology Act, 2000 would require to be amended as the existing provisions were created with paper currency in mind.

There will be a need for strong cooperation between different government agencies and regulatory bodies so that proper checks and balances are created. It seems likely that the roll-out of a digital rupee would be very gradual. The entire world would be eagerly awaiting the launch of India's digital rupee and the precise shape that it takes. For, India has a unique scenario of increasing proliferation of digital payments, coupled with sustained interest in usage of cash. As per present indications, a digital rupee is unlikely to replace cash usage. The high currency to GDP ratio, if switched to digital, would certainly cut the cost of printing, transporting, storing and distributing currency.

Endnote

The sovereignty enjoyed by paper currency for nearly two centuries is now being threatened like never before. The digital rupee is now around the corner. The exact contours and specifications of the digital rupee (currency) would be known in due course. But one thing is certain: it would pose a very strong challenge to paper currency in the years to come. Though paper currency has had a glorious past and a formidable present, its future appears rather uncertain.

With this, we come to the end of our journey. We hope that you, the reader, enjoyed reading this story as much as we did narrating it. Paper currency in India has come a long way since modest beginnings in the colonial times. The eventful journey, full of numerous changes is now poised at a crucial juncture. What lies in store in the decades to come is in the realm of the unknown. But it is obvious that the future is bound to be very different from the past. As the Concept Note on CBDC issued by the Reserve Bank of India in October, 2022 states, "We are at the forefront of a watershed movement in the evolution of currency that will decisively change the very nature of money and its functions."[272] *One thing is certain: the excitement would continue!*

Appendix I

GOVERNORS OF THE RESERVE BANK OF INDIA

Sr. No.	Name	Tenure
1	Sir Osborne Smith	1.4.1935 to 30.6.1937
2	Sir James Braid Taylor	1.7.1937 to 17.2.1943
3	Sir C. D. Deshmukh	11.8.1943 to 30.6.1949
4	Sir Benegal Rama Rau	1.7.1949 to 14.1.1957
5	Shri K. G. Ambegaonkar	14.1.1957 to 28.2.1957
6	Shri H. V. R. Iyengar	1.3.1957 to 28.2.1962
7	Shri P. C. Bhattacharya	1.3.1962 to 30.6.1967
8	Shri L. K. Jha	1.7.1967 to 3.5.1970
9	Shri B. N. Adarkar	4.5.1970 to 15.6.1970
10	Shri S. Jagannathan	16.6.1970 to 19.5.1975
11	Shri N. C. Sen Gupta	19.5.1975 to 19.8.1975
12	Shri K. R. Puri	20.8.1975 to 2.5.1977
13	Shri M. Narasimham	2.5.1977 to 30.11.1977
14	Dr. I. G. Patel	1.12.1977 to 15.9.1982
15	Dr. Manmohan Singh	16.9.1982 to 14.1.1985
16	Shri Amitav Ghosh	15.1.1985 to 4.2.1985
17	Shri R. N. Malhotra	4.2.1985 to 22.12.1990
18	Shri S. Venkitaramanan	22.12.1990 to 21.12.1992
19	Dr. C. Rangarajan	22.12.1992 to 22.11.1997
20	Dr. Bimal Jalan	22.11.1997 to 6.9.2003
21	Dr. Y. V. Reddy	6.9.2003 to 5.9.2008

22	Dr. D. Subbarao	5.9.2008 to 4.9.2013
23	Dr. Raghuram Rajan	4.9.2013 to 4.9.2016
24	Dr. Urjit R. Patel	4.9.2016 to 11.12.2018
25	Shri Shaktikanta Das	12.12.2018 to 10.12.2024
26	Shri Sanjay Malhotra	11.12.2024 to present

Appendix II

CURRENCY MANAGEMENT – INSTITUTIONAL SET-UP

Reserve Bank of India

Department of Currency Management

Currency management is a core function of the Reserve Bank of India. The Department of Currency Management, located in the Central Office of the Bank in Mumbai, plays a key role in meeting the legitimate demand of the public for banknotes and coins by ensuring continuous supply and circulation of notes and coins of various denominations across the country.

The main functions of the department are:

a. Issue of banknotes and putting into circulation coins issued by the Government of India;
b. Estimation of demand for banknotes and coins, determination of design of banknotes in consultation with the Government of India and extend support to the Government for periodic up-gradation of security features;
c. Review the infrastructure and manpower needs in relation to currency management;
d. Managing logistics of currency management for distribution of banknotes and coins and withdrawal and destruction of unfit notes to achieve the objectives of Clean Note Policy;
e. Ensure availability of banknotes and coins related services at banks;

f. Frame policy on security arrangements at Issue Offices and Currency Chests and monitor its implementation;
g. Address the problems relating to counterfeit notes through enhancement of banknote security, strengthening the system of banknote processing and detection of counterfeit banknotes in banks and creating awareness in the public on the features of genuine Indian banknotes;
h. Liaise with the Government and other stakeholders in matters relating to currency management.[273]

The Department of Currency Management was created in the Reserve Bank of India in 1980-81 as an independent unit when the erstwhile Department of Accounts and Expenditure was reorganised into three departments (the other two departments being Department of Expenditure and Budgetary Control and Department of Government and Bank Accounts.) The department is headed by a Chief General Manager (in-Charge) who is assisted by a team of General Managers, Deputy General Managers and other officers and staff.

Issue Department

The Issue Department is the Regional Office of the Department of Currency Management, located at the following 19 centres in the country: Ahmedabad, Belapur (Navi Mumbai), Bengaluru, Bhopal, Bhubaneswar, Chandigarh, Chennai, Guwahati, Hyderabad, Jaipur, Jammu, Kanpur, Kolkata, Lucknow, Mumbai, Nagpur, New Delhi, Patna and Thiruvanantapuram. Each Issue Department is headed by a General Manager or Deputy General Manager who is assisted by a team of officers and staff.

The Issue Department carries out the actual mandate given by Department of Currency Management by implementing the policies and processes as prescribed. The department carries out its tasks on the basis of a codified Manual, called the Issue Department Manual.

Government of India

In the Union Government, the Ministry of Finance, Department of Economic Affairs is entrusted with matters relating to currency. There is a Coin and Currency Division within the department for this work. It is headed by a Director, who is assisted by a Joint Director, Under Secretaries, other officers and staff.

The Division is responsible for matters relating to[274]:

a. Currency, which includes (i) matters relating to design, form and material of currency notes/banknotes; (ii) matters relating to security features of the banknotes; (iii) preparation of SOPs in connection with production and transportation of banknotes; (iv) currency related legislation; (v) indigenization of bank notes production items; (vi) distribute/complaint in respect of supply of material of printing of bank notes and other security products; (vii) expansion, upgradation and modernization of Presses, Paper Mills, Ink factory etc.; (viii) FICN (Fake Indian Currency Notes) related matters; (ix) matters relating to new rupee symbol; (x) matters relating to postal stamp; revenue stamp, passports, etc. including raw material, machinery and equipment; (xi) fair price determination of bank notes and postal stamps; (xii) production planning of printing of currency notes and other security documents; (xiii) pre-shipment inspection of CWBN (Cylinder mode vat made Watermarked Bank Note)/security paper and currency conferences etc.; (xiv) demonetisation; and (xv) court cases post demonetisation;
b. Coins, which includes (i) policy formulation regarding design, shape and size of circulation coins; (ii) fixation of fair prices of coins; (iii) coins related legislations; and (iv) commemorative coins;

c. Digitalisation and Digital Currency, which includes (i) crypto currency and other currency surrogates; (ii) incentivisation of electronic transactions, (iii) virtual currency/ Bitcoin; and (iv) digitisation of the Payment Systems;
d. Security Printing and Minting Corporation of India Limited, which includes (i) administrative control of SPMCIL; (ii) appointment to Board Level posts in SPMCIL; (iii) residual establishment matters of the nine Units of SPMCIL; (iv) court cases filed by the employees of the 9 units of SPMCIL, where Union of India is a party; (v) coordination matters; (vi) coordination of meetings of SPMCIL Board, SPMCIL Pension Fund Trust, etc.; (vii) MoU with SPMCIL; and (viii) preparation of Annual Report of SPMCIL.

The division also deals with matters relating to payment systems and promotion of digital payments.

Appendix III

SALIENT FEATURES OF MG (NEW) SERIES OF NOTES

The salient features of notes in different denominations in the Mahatma Gandhi (New) Series are as given below.

₹2,000 Denomination[275]

Size: 66 mm x 166 mm
Base colour: Magenta

Obverse

1. See through register with denominational numeral 2000
2. Latent image with denominational numeral 2000
3. Denominational numeral २००० in Devnagari
4. Portrait of Mahatma Gandhi at the centre
5. Micro letters 'RBI' and '2000' on the left side of the banknote
6. Windowed security thread with inscriptions 'भारत', RBI and 2000 on banknotes with colour shift. Colour of the thread changes from green to blue when the note is tilted
7. Guarantee Clause, Governor's signature with Promise Clause and RBI emblem towards right
8. Denominational numeral with Rupee Symbol, ₹2000 in colour changing ink (green to blue) on bottom right
9. Ashoka Pillar emblem on the right, Mahatma Gandhi portrait and electrotype (2000) watermarks
10. Number panel with numerals growing from small to big on the top left side and bottom right side

11. For visually impaired, intaglio or raised printing of Mahatma Gandhi portrait, Ashoka Pillar emblem, and identity mark, horizontal rectangle with ₹2000 in raised print on the right, seven angular bleed lines on left and right side in raised print

Reverse

12. Year of printing of the note on the left
13. Swachh Bharat logo with slogan
14. Language panel towards the centre
15. Motif of Mangalayan
16. Denominational numeral २००० in Devnagari

₹500 Denomination[276]

Size: 66 mm x150 mm
Base colour: Stone grey

Obverse

1. See through register with denominational numeral 500
2. Latent image with denominational numeral 500
3. Denominational numeral ५०० in Devnagari
4. Portrait of Mahatma Gandhi at the centre
5. Micro letters 'RBI' and '500' on the left side of the banknote
6. Windowed security thread with inscriptions 'भारत' and RBI with colour shift. Colour of the thread changes from green to blue when the note is tilted
7. Guarantee Clause, Governor's signature with Promise Clause and RBI emblem towards right
8. Denominational numeral with Rupee Symbol, ₹500 in colour changing ink (green to blue) on bottom right
9. Ashoka Pillar emblem on the right, Mahatma Gandhi portrait and electrotype (500) watermarks
10. Number panel with numerals growing from small to big on the top left side and bottom right side

11. For visually impaired, intaglio or raised printing of Mahatma Gandhi portrait, Ashoka Pillar emblem, and identity mark, circle with ₹500 in raised print on the right, five angular bleed lines on left and right side in raised print

Reverse

12. Year of printing of the note on the left
13. Swachh Bharat logo with slogan
14. Language panel
15. Motif of Red Fort with Indian flag
16. Denominational numeral ५०० in Devnagari

₹200 Denomination[277]

Size: 66 mm x 146 mm
Base colour: Bright yellow

Obverse

1. See through register with denominational numeral 200
2. Latent image with denominational numeral 200
3. Denominational numeral २०० in Devnagari
4. Portrait of Mahatma Gandhi at the centre
5. Micro letters 'RBI', 'भारत', 'India' and '200'
6. Windowed security thread with inscriptions 'भारत' and RBI with colour shift.
   Colour of the thread changes from green to blue when the note is tilted
7. Guarantee Clause, Governor's signature with Promise Clause and RBI emblem towards right of Mahatma Gandhi portrait
8. Denominational numeral with Rupee Symbol, ₹ 200 in colour changing ink (green to blue) on bottom right
9. Ashoka Pillar emblem on the right
10. Mahatma Gandhi portrait and electrotype (200) watermarks

11. Number panel with numerals growing from small to big on the top left side and bottom right side
12. For visually impaired

Intaglio or raised printing of Mahatma Gandhi portrait, Ashoka Pillar emblem, raised Identification mark H with micro-text ₹200, four angular bleed lines with two circles in between the lines both on the right and left sides

Reverse

13. Year of printing of the note on the left
14. Swachh Bharat logo with slogan
15. Language panel
16. Motif of Sanchi Stupa
17. Denominational numeral २०० in Devnagari

₹100 Denomination[278]

Size: 66 mm × 142 mm
Base Colour: Lavender

Obverse

1. See through register with denominational numeral 100
2. Latent image with denominational numeral 100
3. Denominational numeral १०० in Devnagari
4. Portrait of Mahatma Gandhi at the centre
5. Micro letters ‘RBI’, ‘भारत’, ‘India’ and ‘100
6. Windowed security thread with inscriptions ‘भारत’ and RBI with colour shift, colour of the thread changes from green to blue when the note is tilted
7. Guarantee Clause, Governor’s signature with Promise Clause and RBI emblem towards right of Mahatma Gandhi portrait
8. Ashoka Pillar emblem on the right
9. Mahatma Gandhi portrait and electrotype (100) watermarks

10. Number panel with numerals in ascending font on the top left side and bottom right side
11. For visually impaired, intaglio or raised printing of Mahatma Gandhi portrait, Ashoka Pillar emblem, raised triangular identification mark with micro-text 100, four angular bleed lines both on the right and left sides

Reverse

12. Year of printing of the note on the left
13. Swachh Bharat logo with slogan
14. Language panel
15. Motif of Rani Ki Vav
16. Denominational numeral १०० in Devnagari

₹50 Denomination[279]

Size: 66 mm x 135 mm
Base Colour: Fluorescent Blue

Obverse

1. See through register with denominational numeral 50
2. Denominational numeral ५० in Devnagari
3. Portrait of Mahatma Gandhi at the centre
4. Micro letters 'RBI', 'भारत', 'INDIA' and '50'
5. Windowed demetalised security thread with inscriptions 'भारत' and RBI
6. Guarantee Clause, Governor's signature with Promise Clause and RBI emblem towards right of Mahatma Gandhi portrait
7. Ashoka Pillar emblem on the right
8. Mahatma Gandhi portrait and electrotype (50) watermarks
9. Number panel with numerals growing from small to big on the top left side and bottom right side

Reverse

10. Year of printing of the note on the left
11. Swachh Bharat logo with slogan
12. Language panel
13. Motif of Hampi with Chariot
14. Denominational numeral ५० in Devnagari

₹20 Denomination[280]

Size: 63 mm x 129 mm
Base colour: Greenish yellow

Obverse

1. See through register with denominational numeral 20
2. Denominational numeral २० in Devnagari
3. Portrait of Mahatma Gandhi at the centre
4. Micro letters 'RBI', 'भारत', 'INDIA' and '20'
5. Windowed demetalised security thread with inscriptions 'भारत' and RBI
6. Guarantee Clause, Governor's signature with Promise Clause and RBI emblem towards right of Mahatma Gandhi portrait
7. Ashoka Pillar emblem on the right
8. Mahatma Gandhi portrait and electrotype (20) watermarks
9. Number panel with numerals growing from small to big on the top left side and bottom right side.

Reverse

10. Year of printing of the note on the left
11. Swachh Bharat logo with slogan
12. Language panel
13. Motif of Ellora Caves
14. Denominational numeral २० in Devnagari.

₹10 Denomination[281]

Size: 63 mm x 123 mm
Base colour: Chocolate brown

Obverse

1. See through register with denominational numeral 10
2. Denominational numeral १० in Devnagari
3. Portrait of Mahatma Gandhi at the centre
4. Micro letters 'RBI', 'भारत', 'INDIA' and '10'
5. Windowed demetalised security thread with inscriptions 'भारत' and RBI
6. Guarantee Clause, Governor's signature with Promise Clause and RBI emblem towards right of Mahatma Gandhi portrait
7. Ashoka Pillar emblem on the right
8. Mahatma Gandhi portrait and electrotype (10) watermarks
9. Number panel with numerals growing from small to big on the top left side and bottom right side

Reverse

10. Year of printing of the note on the left
11. Swachh Bharat logo with slogan
12. Language panel
13. Motif of Sun Temple, Konark
14. Denominational numeral १० in Devnagari

Appendix IV

PARAMETERS FOR PAYMENT OF MUTILATED NOTES

The Reserve Bank of India (Note Refund) Rules, 2009 [as Amended by Reserve Bank of India (Note Refund) Amendment Rules, 2018] provide for rules under which payment of value can be made in respect of mutilated notes.

Notes of denomination ₹1, 2, 5, 10 and 20

Denomination	Length (cm)	Width (cm)	Area (in cm^2)	Minimum area (in cm^2) required for payment of full value*
(1)	**(2)**	**(3)**	**(4)**	**(5)**
1	9.7	6.3	61.11	31
2	10.7	6.3	67.41	34
5	11.7	6.3	73.71	37
10	13.7	6.3	86.31	44
10 (New MG Series)	12.3	6.3	77.49	39
20	14.7	6.3	92.61	47
20 (New MG Series)	12.9	6.3	81.27	41

*Indicated as the next complete higher square centimetre after half of the area of the notes in a particular denomination.";

Notes of denomination ₹50, 100, 200, 500 and 2,000

Denomination	Length (cm)	Width (cm)	Area (in cm^2)	Minimum area (in cm^2) required for payment of full value@	Minimum area (in cm^2) required for payment of half value**
(1)	(2)	(3)	(4)	(5)	(6)
50	14.7	7.3	107.31	86	43
50 (New MG Series)	13.5	6.6	89.10	72	36
100	15.7	7.3	114.61	92	46
100 (New MG Series)	14.2	6.6	93.72	75	38
200	14.6	6.6	96.36	78	39
500	15.0	6.6	99.00	80	40
2000	16.6	6.6	109.56	88	44

@ Rounded off to the next complete higher square centimetre of 80% of the area of the notes in a particular denomination.

** Rounded off to the next complete higher square centimetre of 40% of the area of the notes in a particular denomination.".

The same parameters are applicable to mismatched and imperfect notes too.

Appendix V

CONCEPT NOTE ON CENTRAL BANK DIGITAL CURRENCY

This is the concluding chapter of the Concept Note on Central Bank Digital Currency (CBDC) released by the Reserve Bank of India in October, 2022.

Chapter 8: Way Forward[282]

8.1 RBI has been exploring the pros and cons of introduction of the CBDCs for some time. As there are multiple compelling motivations for the introduction of CBDCs, RBI is currently engaged in working towards a phased implementation strategy, going step by step through various stages of pilots followed by the final launch, and simultaneously examining use cases that could be implemented with minimal or no disruption. Depending on the different use cases, multiple technological options shall be tested and based on the outcomes, the final architecture shall be decided. As per recommendations of the internal Working Group (WG) set up by Reserve Bank in October 2020, RBI is exploring the option of implementation of account-based CBDC in Wholesale segment and token-based CBDC in Retail segment vide a graded approach.

8.2 This phase involves the following steps:

i. Build a prototype as per the recommendations of the WG. Specify technical requirements to technology partners.
ii. Test the idea in an operationally controlled environment to examine its functionality, including the design, deployment plan and success criteria.

iii. Perform test cases with both positive and negative scenarios to examine its durability and document the results.
iv. Evaluate Test Results and finalise the design of the prototype.
v. *Pilot:* Conducting large scale pilots with a diverse and larger user base. Participants of the pilots must include users from different income levels, literacy levels, regions, genders and age groups. This will help RBI understand the potential use of the CBDC in a diverse country like India. The results and learnings of the pilot need to be carefully evaluated and must be incorporated into the final design of the CBDC.

8.3 The recommendations of internal high-level committee on CBDC facilitated firming up views on the issues of motivation for introduction of CBDC, its design features, choice of technology platforms, its implications on policy issues, and a way forward.

8.4 It will be incumbent on RBI to continue monitoring CBDC developments around the world while staying abreast of and potentially contributing to research and technical experimentation. This shall facilitate to stay up to date with the latest research, trends and findings related to CBDC, including those that can affect the economy and design policy measures to address the reputational risk associated with widely available retail CBDC.

8.5 The Bank is deliberating on the various aspects of technological choices available, which includes, suitability of Tech Architecture(DLT/ Centralized/ Hybrid; Open Source/Proprietary), security of the Token Creation Process and Central Bank Node, standards and protocols to be followed by each stakeholder, robust preventive counterfeiting tech choices (Robustness of Verifier technology), security considerations; especially in offline transactions and smart contract features and its use cases in CBDC in both, Wholesale(W) and Retail(R) segment.

8.6 It is envisaged to continue the ongoing CBDC research through:

i. Accessing online resources that compile and share research publicly

ii. Attending international meetings, discussions and working groups related to CBDC
iii. Engaging with international organisations such as the BIS, IMF, World Economic Forum and other standard setting bodies.
iv. Developing bilateral relationships with CBDC research teams around the world.
v. Engaging with all stakeholders including academicians, technology providers.

8.7 Conclusion

CBDC, the central bank digital currency, holds a lot of promises by way of ensuring transparency, and low cost of operation among other benefits and the potential to expand the existing payment systems to address the needs of a wider category of users.

CBDC, across the world, is in conceptual, development, or at pilot stages. Therefore, in the absence of a precedence, extensive stakeholder consultation along with iterative technology design must take place to develop a solution that meets the requirements. While the intent of CBDC and the expected benefits are well understood, it is important to identify innovative methods and compelling use cases that will make CBDC as attractive as cash if not more.

This Concept Note provides a high-level view of motivations for the introduction of CBDC in India, its potential design features, implications on various policy issues, and the possible requirements of a technology platform. Inferences drawn here are exploratory in nature though they appear to be most suitable at this juncture.

The way forward stated in this Concept Note requires elaborate planning in terms of scope, cost, and timelines to ensure the timely roll out of different phases of CBDC introduction.

Endnotes

1 *https://m.rbi.org.in/scripts/FAQView.aspx?Id=136#:~:text=The%20promissory%20clause%20printed%20on,holder%20of%20the%20bank%20note* Reserve Bank of India, FAQs, accessed on May 20, 2022

2 *https://rbidocs.rbi.org.in/rdocs/Speeches/PDFs/CBDC22072021414F2690E7764E13BFD41DF6E50AE0AE.PDF* Central Bank Digital Currency – Is This the Future of Money, Speech delivered by T. Rabi Sankar, Deputy Governor, Reserve Bank of India at New Delhi, July 22, 2021, p.1, accessed on May 20, 2022

3 Picture taken from https://pbs.twimg.com/media/FJK9kknXoAUbRFt.jpg

4 *https://dbpedia.org/page/Jiaozi_(currency),* accessed on May 20, 2022

5 *https://en.wikipedia.org/wiki/Banknote*, accessed on May 20, 2022

6 *https://rbidocs.rbi.org.in/rdocs/Speeches/PDFs/CBDC22072021414F2690E7764E13BFD41DF6E50AE0AE.PDF* Central Bank Digital Currency – Is This the Future of Money, Speech delivered by T. Rabi Sankar, Deputy Governor, Reserve Bank of India at New Delhi, July 22, 2021, p.2, accessed on May 20, 2022

7 *Ibid.*, p.2

8 Reserve Bank of India (2024) *Annual Report 2023-24,* p.236, 224

9 Shaikh, Bazil and Sandhya Srinivasan (2009), *The Paper & The Promise,* Reserve Bank of India, Department of Currency Management, Mumbai, p.15

10 https://www.spink.com/media/view?id=48 *Banknotes for the Raj by Dr K.A.Rodgers,* June 8, 2011, accessed on January 24, 2022

11 https://archive.org/details/in.ernet.dli.2015.59394/page/n49/mode/2up *Paper Currency in India by B.B. Das Gupta (1927),* Calcutta University, p.11, accessed on January 24, 2022

12 Picture taken from https://upload.wikimedia.org/wikipedia/commons/thumb/4/4b/Bank_of_ Hindostan_-_Sixteen_Sicca_Rupees.jpg/220px-Bank_of_Hindostan_-_Sixteen_Sicca_Rupees.jpg

13 Shaikh, Bazil and Sandhya Srinivasan (2009), *The Paper & The Promise,* Reserve Bank of India, Department of Currency Management, Mumbai, p.17

14 *Ibid.*, p.17

15 https://archive.org/details/in.ernet.dli.2015.59394/page/n49/mode/2up *Paper Currency in India by B.B. Das Gupta (1927),* Calcutta University, p.20, accessed on January 24, 2022

16 Shaikh, Bazil and Sandhya Srinivasan (2009), *The Paper & The Promise,* Reserve Bank of India, Department of Currency Management, Mumbai, p.18

17 *Ibid.*,p.19

18 Picture taken from https://upload.wikimedia.org/wikipedia/commons/thumb/5/51/ Bank_of_Bombay%2C_10_Rupees_note%2C_1860.jpg/800px-Bank_of_Bombay%2C_10_Rupees _note%2C_1860.jpg?20180701193604

19 Weintraub, Charles and Kurt Schuler (2013) *India's Paper Currency Department (1862-1935) as a Quasi Currency Board,* Studies in Applied Economics, No.9, December, p.3

20 https://www.spink.com/media/view?id=48 *Banknotes for the Raj by Dr K.A.Rodgers,* June 8, 2011, and https://www.rbi.org.in/Scripts/pm_britishindia.aspx *Reserve Bank of India, Currency Museum, British India Issues,* accessed on January 24, 2022

21 Picture taken from https://www.rbi.org.in/Scripts/pm_britishindia.aspx *Reserve Bank of India, Currency Museum, British India Issues,* accessed on January 24, 2022

22 Ambedkar, B.R. (1947) *History of Indian Currency & Banking,* Thacker and Company Limited, Bombay, p.53

23 Weintraub, Charles and Kurt Schuler (2013) *India's Paper Currency Department (1862-1935) as a Quasi Currency Board,* Studies in Applied Economics, No.9, December, p.6

24 https://www.livehistoryindia.com/story/eras/indias-first-currency-note *India's First Currency Note by Krutika Haraniya, October 5, 2018,* accessed on July 1, 2022

25 https://rbi.org.in/Scripts/pm_britishindia.aspx *Reserve Bank of India, Currency Museum, British India Issues,* accessed on January 26, 2022

26 https://indianexpress.com/article/research/a-century-ago-india-got-its-rare-and-strange-rs-2-5-note-5008328/#:~:text=Courtesy%3A%20Todywalla%20auctions *A century ago, India got its rare, and strange, Rs 2.5 note by Nandini Rathi, The Indian Express, January3, 2018,* accessed on January 26, 2022

27 Picture taken from https://encrypted-tbn0.gstatic.com/images?q=tbn: ANd9G cSXANWFG2X7 guzKqqxEPQwXL8-jXBmgzDKO0Q&usqp=CAU, accessed on January 26, 2022

28 Shaikh, Bazil and Sandhya Srinivasan (2009), *The Paper & The Promise,* Reserve Bank of India, Department of Currency Management, Mumbai, p.28

29 *Ibid.*, p.28

30 Weintraub, Charles and Kurt Schuler (2013) *India's Paper Currency Department (1862-1935) as a Quasi Currency Board*, Studies in Applied Economics, No.9, December, p.7

31 https://rbi.org.in/Scripts/pm_cashcoupons.aspx *Reserve Bank of India, Currency Museum, Emergency Issues Princely States: Cash Coupons,* accessed on January 26, 2022

32 http://indianbanknote.blogspot.com/2010/06/paper-money-of-jammu-kashmir-india.html *Paper Money of Jammu & Kashmir posted by Rezwan Razack on June 25, 2010,* accessed on July 10, 2022

33 Picture taken from https://www.mintageworld.com/blog/wp-content/uploads/2017/11/Feature-Image-copy-1.jpg, accessed on July 10, 2022

34 Picture taken from https://upload.wikimedia.org/wikipedia/commons/thumb/4/41/Five-rupee_note_from_Hyderabad.jpg/250px-Five-rupee_note_from_Hyderabad.jpg

35 https://rbi.org.in/Scripts/pm_cashcoupons.aspx *Reserve Bank of India, Currency Museum, Emergency Issues Princely States: Cash Coupons,* accessed on January 26, 2022

36 Shaikh, Bazil and Sandhya Srinivasan (2009), *The Paper & The Promise,* Reserve Bank of India, Department of Currency Management, Mumbai, p.73

37 https://drs.nio.org/drs/bitstream/handle/2264/143/Portuguese-%20Puri-paper% 20Note.pdf? sequence=1 *Depiction of Jagannath Temple of Puri on the Portuguese Paper Currency by Sila Tripathi, Studies in History and Culture, Vol.8, Nos. 1&2, 2003,* accessed on June 12, 2022

38 *Ibid.*, accessed on June 12, 2022

39 Shaikh, Bazil and Sandhya Srinivasan (2009), *The Paper & The Promise,* Reserve Bank of India, Department of Currency Management, Mumbai, p.73

40 Picture taken from https://3.bp.blogspot.com/-QCWDHYqf6k4/UMwdvwrULBI/AAAAAAAAK58/Q6dzo4JYEZw/w1200-h630-p-k-no-nu/Banco+Nacional+Ultramarino+Banknotes+Portuguese+India.jpg, accessed on July 10, 2022

41 Picture taken from https://dygtyjqp7pi0m.cloudfront.net/i/28832/25109170_1.jpg?v=8D3AD8F89EDE610, accessed on July 10, 2022

42 https://rbi.org.in/Scripts/pm_indofrench.aspx *Reserve Bank of India, Currency Museum, Indo-French Issues,* accessed on January 26, 2022

43 Simha, S.L.N. (1970) *History of the Reserve Bank of India, Vol. I, 1935-1951*, Reserve Bank of India, Mumbai, p.26

44 *Ibid.*, p.27

45 *Ibid.*, p.27

46 *Ibid.*, p.37

47 *Ibid.*, p.38-39

48 *Ibid.*, p.123

49 *Ibid.*, p.132

50 Picture taken from https://marudhar-arts.s3.ap-south-.amazonaws.com/uploads/t/2022/ 2022077910.jpg, accessed on January 15, 2023

51 Simha, S.L.N. (1970) *History of the Reserve Bank of India, Vol. I, 1935-1951*, Reserve Bank of India, Mumbai, p.328

52 Shaikh, Bazil and Sandhya Srinivasan (2009) *The Paper & The Promise*, Department of Currency Management, Reserve Bank of India, Mumbai, p.35

53 Picture taken from https://marudhar-arts.s3.ap-south1.amazonaws.com/uploads/l/1018/ 1018007013.jpg, accessed on January 15, 2023

54 Simha, S.L.N. (1970) *History of the Reserve Bank of India, Vol. I, 1935-1951*, Reserve Bank of India, Mumbai, p.550

55 Shaikh, Bazil and Sandhya Srinivasan (2009) *The Paper & The Promise*, Department of Currency Management, Reserve Bank of India, Mumbai, p.63

56 *Ibid.*, p.65

57 *Ibid.*, p.43

58 https://www.rbi.org.in/Scripts/pm_republicindia.aspx *Reserve Bank of India, Currency Museum, Republic India Issues,* accessed on January 26, 2022

59 *Ibid.*, accessed on January 26, 2022

60 Bajoria, Rahul (2018) *The Story of the Reserve Bank of India*, Rupa Publications India Pvt. Ltd. New Delhi, p.57

61 Reserve Bank of India (2005) *The Reserve Bank of India 1968-1981 Vol.3*, p.440

62 Balachandran, G. (1998) *The Reserve Bank of India 1951-1967,* Reserve Bank of India, p.749

63 https://rbi.org.in/Scripts/pm_republicindia.aspx, *Reserve Bank of India, Currency Museum, Republic India Issues,* accessed on January 26, 2022

64 Reserve Bank of India (2013) *The Reserve Bank of India, Volume 4 (1981-1997),* Academic Foundation, New Delhi, p.1044

65 Shaikh, Bazil and Sandhya Srinivasan (2009) *The Paper & The Promise,* Department of Currency Management, Reserve Bank of India, Mumbai, p.85

66 https://www.thebetterindia.com/35477/gandhi-image-on-currency-notes/ *So This Is Where the Picture of Gandhi on Currency Notes Came From by Tanaya Singh Oct 2, 2015,* accessed on January 26, 2022

67 Reserve Bank of India (2005) *Press Release: 2005-06/315,* September 10

68 https://rbi.org.in/Scripts/pm_republicindia.aspx *Reserve Bank of India, Currency Museum, Republic India Issues,* accessed on January 26, 2022

69 Picture taken from the collection of Rajesh Seth

70 https://www.mintageworld.com/blog/journey-one-rupee-note/ *Mintage World, Blog, The Journey of One Rupee Note,* accessed on July 10, 2022

71 Shaikh, Bazil and Sandhya Srinivasan (2009) *The Paper & The Promise,* Department of Currency Management, Reserve Bank of India, Mumbai, p.50

72 Nachane, D.M. *et al* (2013) *Modelling Currency Demand in India: An Empirical Study,* Reserve Bank of India, Department of Economic and Policy Research, Mumbai, DRG Study No 39, p.4

73 Reserve Bank Staff College (2020) *Reserve Bank of India: Functions and Working,* p.138

74 *Ibid.*, p.137

75 https://cnpnashik.spmcil.com/Interface/History_cnpnashik.aspx?menue=1, accessed on April 23, 2022

76 *Ibid.*, accessed on April 23, 2022

77 Picture taken from https://www.todywallaauctions.com/Article2.aspx, accessed on February 8, 2022

78 https://cnpnashik.spmcil.com/Interface/History_cnpnashik.aspx?menue=1, accessed on April 23, 2022

79 https://www.todywallaauctions.com/Article2.aspx *The Security Press, Currency Note Press, Mints and Security Paper Mill of India by Rezwan Razack,* accessed on February 8, 2022

80 Security Printing and Minting Corporation of India Limited, *Annual Report 2021*

81 Reserve Bank of India (2013) *The Reserve Bank of India 1981-1997 Volume 4*, Academic Foundation, New Delhi, p.1044

82 Reserve Bank of India (1997) *Annual Report 1996-97*, p.146

83 Lok Sabha Secretariat, New Delhi (April 2010) *Sixth Report Committee on Public Undertakings 2009-10 Security Printing and Minting Corporation of India Limited, Ministry of Finance (Department of Economic Affairs)*, p.42

84 *Ibid.*, p.65

85 Reserve Bank of India (2001) *Annual Report 2000-01*, para 12.12

86 Reserve Bank of India (2024) *Annual Report 2023-24*, p.157

87 Balachandran, G. (1998) *The Reserve Bank of India 1951-1967*, Reserve Bank of India, p.755

88 *Ibid.*, p.756

89 Reserve Bank of India (2010) *Press Release: 2009-10/1269*, March 22

90 *Ibid.*, March 22

91 Lok Sabha Secretariat, New Delhi (April 2010) *Sixth Report Committee on Public Undertakings 2009-10 Security Printing and Minting Corporation of India Limited, Ministry of Finance (Department of Economic Affairs)*

92 https://datais.info/loksabha/question/4ac9dc1f5438129063402c3ce39160f6/PRINTING+OF+CURRENCY+NOTES/, accessed on April 6, 2022

93 Ministry of Finance, Government of India, *Annual Report 2020-21*, p.70

94 Based on The Hindu Business Line, February 14, 2020 *Why isn't India using polymer notes by Ganga Narayan Rath* https://www.thehindubusinessline.com/opinion/why-isnt-india-using-polymer-banknotes/ article30812668.ece, accessed on April 12, 2022 and *Annual Reports of Reserve Bank of India*

95 Reserve Bank of India (2020) *Annual Report 2019-20*, p.183

96 Reserve Bank Staff College (2020) *Reserve Bank of India: Functions and Working*, p.136

97 Reserve Bank of India (2021) *Annual Report 2020-21*, p.183

98 Figure derived from data from Annual Report of Reserve Bank of India 2021-22, p.169-170

99 Figure derived from data from Annual Report of Reserve bank of India 2014-15, p.109-110

100 The Hindu Business Line, March 9, 2021 *https://www.thehindubusinessline.com/money-and-banking/50-500-notes-now-cheaper-to-print-10-20-100-pricier/article34021926.ece*, accessed on Jan 28, 2022

101 The Hindu, July 3, 2015 *https://www.thehindu.com/news/national/cost-of-printing-a-onerupee-note-is-rs-114/article7378821.ece*, accessed on Jan 28, 2022

102 http://indianbanknote.blogspot.com/2010/03/prefix-inset-and-serial-number-syntax.html#:~:text=As%20in%20the%20case%20of,print%20notes%20for%20the%20RBI, *Prefix, Inset and Serial Number Syntax of Mahatma Gandhi Banknotes of India by Rezwan Razack, March 22, 2010,* accessed on July 10, 2022

103 Reserve Bank of India (2006) *Circular RBI/2005-06/375 DCM (Plg) No. G-48 /10.01.08/2005-06, April 26*

104 Balachandran, G. (1998) *The Reserve Bank of India 1951-1967,* Reserve Bank of India p.750-751

105 Based on *Reserve Bank of India: Functions and Working (2020),* Reserve Bank Staff College, Chennai, p.142-143

106 Reserve Bank of India (2020) *Press Release 2019-20/1570,* Jan 1

107 Business Standard, February 13, 2020 *https://www.business-standard.com/article/pti-stories/daffodil-software-uses-ai-to-empower-the-visually-impaired-in-rbi-mani-app-120021300446_1.html,* accessed on February 4, 2022

108 Reserve Bank of India (2024) *Annual Report 2023-24,* p.160

109 Reserve Bank of India (2024) *Annual Report 2023-24,* p.157

110 Reserve Bank of India (2019) *Minimum Standards for a Currency Chest, RBI/2018-19/166 DCM (CC) No.2482/03.39.01/2018-19,* April 8

111 Simha, S.L.N. (1970) *History of the Reserve Bank of India, Vol. I, 1935-1951,* Reserve Bank of India, Mumbai, p.137

112 Reserve Bank of India, *Annual Report 1990-91,* p.183

113 Roy, Tirthankar (2022) *The Reserve Bank of India, Volume 5, 1997-2008,* p.344

114 Reserve Bank of India, *Annual Report 2023-24,* p.157

115 Reserve Bank of India, *Annual Report 2016-17,* p.125

116 *Ibid.,* p.132

117 https://rbi.org.in/scripts/ATMView.aspx?atmid=86 *ATM, Acceptance Infrastructure and Card Statistics for the month of March 2022,* accessed on December 1, 2022

118 https://www.gi-de.com/en/spotlight/payment/how-long-does-paper-money-last *The lifespan of money Expert Opinion,* accessed on March 20, 2022

119 Reserve Bank of India, *Annual Report 2007-08,* p.271

120 Reserve Bank of India (2002) *Annual Report 2001-02,* p.191

121 Picture taken from https://www.infotechlaos.com/images/product/sorting/DLR-7000-CB.jpg, accessed on July 10, 2022

122 *Ibid.*, p.191

123 *Ibid.*, p.191

124 Picture taken from https://www.infotechlaos.com/images/portfolio/portfolio11.jpg, accessed on July 10, 2022

125 https://www.rediff.com/money/2003/feb/19rbi.htm *Mint St pushes shredded note curios by Ishita Ayan Dutt and Pradeep Gooptu,* February 19, 2003, accessed on February 15, 2022

126 https://ippta.co/wp-content/uploads/2021/01/2009_Issue_3_IPPTA_Articel_06.pdf *Cost Effective Production of Handmade Paper Through Recycling of Shredded Currency Waste of Reserve Bank of India – An Enzymatic Route by Chauhan Sunita, et. al., IPPTA Journal, Vol.21, No.3, July-Sept 2009, p.112,* accessed on August 1, 2022

127 https://www.newindianexpress.com/business/2021/nov/08/five-years-of-demonetisation-how-over-800-tonnes-of-shreddednotes-ended-up-in-south-africa-2380985.html, *New Indian Express, November 8, 2021,* accessed on February 15, 2022

128 Reserve Bank of India, *Annual Report 2020-21,* p.181

129 *Ibid.*, p.182

130 Reserve Bank of India (2019), *The Reserve Bank of India Act, 1934, Section 28,* available at https://rbidocs.rbi.org.in/rdocs/Publications/PDFs/RBIA1934170510.PDF, accessed on February 15, 2022

131 *Ibid.*, Sections 58(1) and 58(2)(q), accessed on February 15,2022

132 Reserve Bank of India (1975), *RBI (Note Refund) Rules, RBI Bulletin, July,* p.501

133 Picture taken from https://cdn.dnaindia.com/sites/default/files/styles/full/public/2022/04/04/1305287-currency-notes.jpg, accessed on February 15, 2022

134 Reserve Bank of India (1975), *RBI (Note Refund) Rules, RBI Bulletin, July,* p.504

135 Reserve Bank of India (2004) *Providing facilities to public for exchange of notes, coins, etc. RBI/2004/19 DCM (NE) No.310/08.07.18/2003-04,* January 19

136 Reserve Bank of India (2013) *Facility for exchange of notes and coins RBI/2012-13/428 DCM (NE) No. 3498 /08.07.18/2012-13,* January 28, available at https://rbidocs.rbi.org.in/rdocs/notification/PDFs/NEC050313FL.pdf , accessed on February 15, 2022

137 Based on Reserve Bank of India (2018) *Reserve Bank of India (Note Refund) Rules, 2009 [as amended by Reserve Bank of India (Note Refund) Amendment Rules 2018]*, available at https://rbidocs.rbi.org.in/rdocs/Publications/PDFs/NRR2812201818E213A335254034A958ACDBED30501B.PDF, accessed on February 15, 2022

138 Reserve Bank of India (1997) *Annual Report 1996-97*, p.146

139 Reserve Bank of India (2022) *Master Circular – Facility for Exchange of Notes and Coins, RBI/2022-23/01DCM (NE) No.G-5/08.07.18/2022-23*, April 1, para 3

140 Based on Reserve Bank of India (2018) *Reserve Bank of India (Note Refund) Rules, 2009 [as amended by Reserve Bank of India (Note Refund) Amendment Rules 2018]*, available at https://rbidocs.rbi.org.in/rdocs/Publications/PDFs/NRR2812201818E213A335254034A958ACDBED30501B.PDF, accessed on February 15, 2022

141 *Ibid.*, accessed on February 15, 2022

142 *Ibid.*, accessed on February 15, 2022

143 Based on Reserve Bank of India (2022) *Master Circular – Facility for Exchange of Notes and Coins RBI/2022-23/01DCM (NE) No.G-5/08.07.18/2022-23*, April 1, para 6

144 Reserve Bank of India (2018) *Reserve Bank of India (Note Refund) Rules, 2009 [as amended by Reserve Bank of India (Note Refund) Amendment Rules 2018]*, available at https://rbidocs.rbi.org.in/rdocs/Publications/PDFs/NRR2812201818E213A335254034A958ACDBED30501B.PDF, p.16

145 Nachane, D.M. *et al* (2013) *Modelling Currency Demand in India: An Empirical Study*, Reserve Bank of India, Department of Economic and Policy Research, Mumbai, DRG Study No 39, p.25

146 Reserve Bank of India (2002) *Handbook of Statistics on Indian Economy, Table 32*, available at *https://rbidocs.rbi.org.in/rdocs/Publications/PDFs/25857.pdf*, accessed on April 30, 2022

147 Reserve Bank of India (2005) *The Reserve Bank of India 1967-1981, Volume 3*, p.431, 433

148 *Ibid.*, p.437

149 Jain, R. K. (2003) *Reserve Bank's Clean Note Policy: An Overview, Reserve Bank of India Occasional Papers, Vol. 24, Nos. 1 and 2, Summer and Monsoon*, p.181

150 Reserve Bank of India (2005) *The Reserve Bank of India 1967-1981, Volume 3*, p.439

151 Jain, R. K. (2003) *Reserve Bank's Clean Note Policy: An Overview, Reserve Bank of India Occasional Papers, Vol. 24, Nos. 1 and 2, Summer and Monsoon,* p.181

152 *Ibid.*, p.181

153 The working of CVPS machines has been described in an earlier chapter.

154 Reserve Bank of India (2003) *Annual Report 2002-03,* p.203

155 The SBS machines have been described in an earlier chapter.

156 Reserve Bank of India (2004) *Annual Report 2003-04,* p.186

157 Reserve Bank of India (2004) *Annual Report 2003-04,* p.201-202

158 *Ibid.*, p.204 and *Annual Report 2004-05,* p.187

159 Reserve Bank of India (2002) *Annual Report 2001-02,* p.191

160 Reserve Bank of India (2003) *Annual Report 2002-03,* p.204

161 Reserve Bank of India (2016) *Annual Report 2015-16,* p.91

162 Reserve Bank of India (1997) *Annual Report 1996-97,* p.146

163 Reserve Bank of India (2001) *Annual Report 2000-01,* para 12.9

164 https://www.financialexpress.com/archive/a-wad-of-notes-till-staples-do-them-apart/52725/ *A Wad Of Notes Till Staples Do Them Apart* Financial Express, July 22, 2002, accessed on April 30, 2022

165 Jain, R. K. (2003) *Reserve Bank's Clean Note Policy: An Overview, Reserve Bank of India Occasional Papers, Vol. 24, Nos. 1 and 2, Summer and Monsoon,* p.185

166 Roy, Tirthankar (2022) *The Reserve Bank of India Volume 5 1997-2008,* Cambridge University Press, p.349

167 Reserve Bank of India (2002) *Annual Report 2001-02,* p.191

168 Roy, Tirthankar (2022) *The Reserve Bank of India Volume 5 1997-2008,* Cambridge University Press, p.349

169 *Ibid.*, p.350

170 Reserve Bank of India (2005) *Annual Report 2004-05,* p.168

171 Reserve Bank of India (2013) *Circular RBI/2012-13/500 DCM (NPD) No.5133/09.39.000/2012-13 dated May 10, 2013,* para 2

172 Reserve Bank of India (2010) *Installation of Note Sorting Machines – Note Authentication and Fitness Sorting Parameters, RBI/2009-10/459, DCM(R&D) No.G-26/18.0014/2009-10,* May 10

173 Reserve Bank of India (2022) *Note Sorting Machines – Authentication and Fitness Sorting Parameters, RBI/2022-23/79, DCM(NPD)No.S488/18.00.14/2022-23,* July 1

174 https://rbidocs.rbi.org.in/rdocs/Speeches/PDFs/SPDGBC22042014.pdf *Currency Management: Issues and Challenges (With special reference to India) Speech delivered by Deputy Governor K.C.Chakraborty at Washington,* April 8, 2014

175 The percentages have been derived from the data available in the Annual Reports of the Reserve Bank of India for the four years 2010-11, 2011-12, 2012-13 and 2013-14

176 Reserve Bank of India (2014) *Circular RBI/2013-14/509 DCM(Plg) No.G-19/3880/10.27.00/2013-14,* March 3, enclosure

177 Prasad, Eswar S. (2021) *The Future of Money, The Belknap Press of Harvard University Press, Cambridge, Massachusetts,* p.218

178 Das Gupta, B. B. (1927) *Paper Currency in India,* Calcutta University, p.11-12

179 Shaikh, Bazil and Sandhya Srinivasan (2009) *The Paper & The Promise,* Department of Currency Management, Reserve Bank of India, Mumbai, p.19

180 *Ibid.,* p.26

181 Das Gupta, B. B. (1927) *Paper Currency in India,* Calcutta University, p.244

182 Shaikh, Bazil and Sandhya Srinivasan (2009) *The Paper & The Promise,* Department of Currency Management, Reserve Bank of India, Mumbai, p.35

183 Reserve Bank of India (1946) *Report on Currency and Finance, 1945-46,* p.116

184 Reserve Bank of India, *Report of the High Level Group on Systems and Procedures for Currency Distribution (August 2009),* p.5

185 *Ibid.,* p.9

186 Reserve Bank of India (2016) *Annual Report 2015-16,* p.92

187 Reserve Bank of India (2017) *Annual Report 2016-17,* p.127

188 Reserve Bank of India (2021) *Annual Report 2020-21,* p.180

189 Reserve Bank of India (2022) *Annual Report 2021-22,* p.170-71

190 National Crime Records Bureau (2022) *Crime in India Statistics 2021 Volume III,* p.1342

191 *Ibid.,* p.1394

192 http://www.ieport.com/2008/customs_not_nt/not43.htm *Notification No. 43/ 2008 – CUSTOM (N.T.) dated 13.5.2008,* accessed on April 15, 2022

193 Bose, Sanjoy and Abhiman Das (March 2013) *Estimation of Counterfeit Currency in India – Alternative Methodologies, RBI Working Paper Series,* Department of Economic and Policy Research, Reserve Bank of India, p.2

194 https://thediplomat.com/2016/11/indias-fight-against-fake-currency/ *India's Fight Against Fake Currency by Sharmad Mahajan,* November 15, 2016, accessed on April 12, 2022

195 *https://timesofindia.indiatimes.com/india/fake-notes-worth-rs-400-crores-in-circulation/articleshow/52214965.cms* Fake notes worth Rs 400 crore in circulation by Neerej Chauhan, Times of India, May 11, 2016, accessed on April 15, 2022

196 *https://pib.gov.in/newsite/PrintRelease.aspx?relid=153404 Prime Minister's Address to the Nation,* Press Information Bureau, Government of India Nov 8, 2016, accessed on April 12, 2022

197 *https://thediplomat.com/2016/11/indias-fight-against-fake-currency/* India's Fight Against Fake Currency by Sharmad Mahajan, November 15, 2016, accessed on April 12, 2022

198 *https://www.eurasiareview.com/05102021-india-ficn-and-counterfeit-assault-analysis/* India: FICN And Counterfeit Assault – Analysis by Ajit Kumar Singh, October 5, 2021, accessed on April 11, 2022

199 Shaikh, Bazil and Sandhya Srinivasan (2009) *The Paper & The Promise,* Department of Currency Management, Reserve Bank of India, Mumbai, p.21

200 Balachandran, G. (1998) *The Reserve Bank of India 1951-1967,* Reserve Bank of India, p.750

201 Roy, Tirthankar (2022) *The Reserve Bank of India Volume 5 1997-2008,* Cambridge University Press, p.362

202 *Ibid.,* p.365

203 Reserve Bank of India (2006) *Annual Report 2005-06,* p.201

204 *https://main.sci.gov.in/jonew/judis/20477.pdf* Supreme Court of India, Case No. Appeal (crl.) 1024 of 2001, Date of Judgement 5/10/2001, accessed on April 15, 2022

205 *https://www.mha.gov.in/MHA1/Par2017/pdfs/par2021-pdfs/LS-27072021/1225.pdf Circulation of Fake Currency, Lok Sabha Unstarred Question No. 1225 answered on July 27, 2021,* para (a) to (d), ii and iii

206 Reserve Bank of India (2022) *Master Circular – Detection and Impounding of Counterfeit Notes RBI/2022-23/07 DCM (FNVD) G –1/16.01.05/2022-23,* April 1, p.2

207 *Ibid.,* p.4

208 Reserve Bank of India (2013) *Detection and Reporting of counterfeit notes RBI/2012-13/562 DCM (FNVD) No.5840/16.01.05/2012-13,* June 27, para 2

209 Reserve Bank of India (2022) *Master Circular – Detection and Impounding of Counterfeit Notes RBI/2022-23/07 DCM (FNVD) G –1/16.01.05/2022-23,* April 1, p.7-8

210 Simha, S.L.N. (1970) *History of the Reserve Bank of India, Vol. I, 1935-1951,* Reserve Bank of India, Mumbai, p.706

211 Picture taken from https://marudhar-arts.s3.ap-south-1.amazonaws.com/uploads/l/2023/2023057013.jpg, accessed on January 2, 2023

212 Simha, S.L.N. (1970) *History of the Reserve Bank of India, Vol. I, 1935-1951,* Reserve Bank of India, Mumbai, p.708

213 *Ibid.*, p.709

214 Singh, Charan (2018) *India since Demonetisation, Working Paper No: 567,* Indian Institute of Management, Bangalore, p.7

215 *https://www.news18.com/news/india/demonetisation-newspaper-headlines-from-1946-tell-a-story-similar-to-2016-1311844.html Demonetisation: Newspaper Headlines from 1946 Tell a Story Similar to 2016 by Soumyadip Choudhury, November 14, 2016,* accessed on April 1, 2022

216 Balachandran, G. (1998) *The Reserve Bank of India 1951-1967,* Reserve Bank of India, p.750

217 Reserve Bank of India (2005) *The Reserve Bank of India 1967-1981, Volume 3,* p.451-452

218 Bajoria, Rahul (2018) *The Story of the Reserve Bank of India*, Rupa Publications India Pvt. Ltd. New Delhi, p.95

219 Picture taken from https://mintage2.s3.amazonaws.com/note/L-1b-f.jpg, accessed on January 2, 2023

220 J Dennis Rajakumar and S L Shetty (2016) *Demonetisation: 1978, the Present and the Aftermath*, Economic and Political Weekly, Vol 51, Issue 48, 26 November https://www.epw.in/journal/2016/48/commentary/demonetisation-1978-present-and-aftermath.html, accessed on February 10, 2022

221 Reserve Bank of India (1978) *Report on Currency and Finance 1977-78,* p.77

222 Reserve Bank of India (2016) *Press Release 2015-16/2941, June 18,* accessed on February 2, 2022

223 *https://pib.gov.in/newsite/PrintRelease.aspx?relid=153404 Prime Minister's Address to the Nation,* Press Information Bureau, Government of India Nov 8, 2016, accessed on January 28, 2022

224 *Ibid.*, accessed on January 28, 2022

225 Ministry of Finance, Government of India, *Annual Report 2016-17,* p.56

226 Reserve Bank of India, *Annual Report 2016-17,* p.132

227 Lahiri, Amartaya (2020) *The Great Indian Demonetisation, Journal of Economic Perspectives, Vol 34, No 1,* p.60 https://www.jstor.org/stable/10.2307/26873529, accessed on April 3, 2022

228 Bajoria, Rahul (2018) *The Story of the Reserve Bank of India,* Rupa Publications India Pvt. Ltd. New Delhi, p.237

229 *https://www.businesstoday.in/industry/banks/story/rbi-warned-govt-about-demonetisation-hours-before-pm-modi-8-pm-announcement-179379-2019-03-11* BusinessToday.In March 11, 2019, accessed on March 10, 2022

230 Rajan, Raghuram G. (2018) *I Do What I Do,* Harper Business, Gurugram, p.xvii

231 Ministry of Finance, Government of India, *Annual Report 2016-17,* p.59

232 Reserve Bank of India, *Annual Report 2016-17,* p.132

233 Singh, Bhupal and Harendra Behera (2017) *Impact of Demonetisation on the Financial Sector,* RBI Bulletin, November, p.8

234 Reserve Bank of India, *Annual Report 2016-17,* p.129

235 Reserve Bank of India, *Annual Report 2017-18,* p.153

236 Ministry of Finance, Government of India, *Annual Report 2017-18,* p.48-49

237 Geethanjali Nataraj (2017) *Demonetisation and its Impact Theme Paper,* Indian Institute of Public Administration, New Delhi https://www.iipa.org.in/new/upload/theme2017.pdf, accessed on March 20, 2022

238 Reserve Bank of India, *Annual Report 2016-17,* p.127,129

239 Lahiri, Amartaya (2020) *The Great Indian Demonetisation, Journal of Economic Perspectives, Vol 34, No 1,* p.67 https://www.jstor.org/stable/10.2307/26873529, accessed on April 3, 2022

240 *http://www.isec.ac.in/WP%20450%20-%20Pratap%20Singh_2%20-%20Final.pdf Demonetisation 2016 and Its Impact on Indian Economy and Taxation by Pratap Singh, Working Paper 450 (2019)* Institute for Social and Economic Change, Bengaluru, accessed on April 10, 2022

241 Subhash Chandra Garg (2021) *5 Years After Demonetisation, Cash & Black Money Are As Much As Earlier,* 8 November https://www.thequint.com/voices/opinion/5-years-after-demonetisation-corruption-black-money-are-as-good-as-ever#read-more, accessed on March 22, 2022

242 *https://www.statista.com/statistics/1028133/india-currency-in-circulation-as-share-of-gdp/ Share of currency in circulation to GDP in India from financial year 2015 to 2022,* accessed on September 1, 2022

243 https://rbidocs.rbi.org.in/rdocs/ATM/PDFs/BATMP140312.pdf *Bank-wise ATM and Card Statistics-January 2012,* accessed on May 31, 2022

244 https://www.rbi.org.in/Scripts/BS_ViewBulletin.aspx?Id=21048 *RBI Bulletin, May 2022,* accessed on August 31, 2022

245 Reserve Bank of India (2022) *Annual Report 2021-22,* p.176

246 Reserve Bank of India (2021) *Master Directions on Prepaid Payment Instruments (PPIs) CO.DPSS.POLC.No. S-479/02.14.006/2021-22 dated August 27, 2021 (Updated as on November 12, 2021),* p.3

247 *Ibid.,* p.3-4

248 Reserve Bank of India (2015) *Annual Report 2014-15,* p.116

249 Reserve Bank of India (2022) *Annual Report 2021-22,* p.176

250 https://www.rbi.org.in/Scripts/BS_ViewBulletin.aspx?Id=21048 *RBI Bulletin, May 2022,* accessed on August 31, 2022

251 Raj, Janak *et al* (2020) *Modelling and Forecasting Currency Demand in India: A Heterodox Approach,* Reserve Bank of India Occasional Papers, Vol. 41, No. 1, 2020, p.8,10

252 *Ibid.,* p.10

253 Reserve Bank of India (2022) *Annual Report 2021-22,* p.290

254 Reserve Bank of India (2022) *Benchmarking India's Payment Systems, Department of Payment and Settlement Systems, Central Office, Mumbai,* p.35

255 Prasad, Eswar S. (2021) *The Future of Money, The Belknap Press of Harvard University Press, Cambridge, Massachusetts,* p.109

256 *Ibid.,* p.131

257 *Ibid.,* p.132

258 Reserve Bank of India (2013) *RBI cautions users of Virtual currencies against risks, Press Release 2013-14/1261 dated December 24, 2013*

259 https://triple-a.io/crypto-ownership-india/ *Cryptocurrency information about India,* accessed on July 1, 2022

260 https://rbidocs.rbi.org.in/rdocs/Speeches/PDFs/CRYPTOCURRENCIESFBEA27DE561D427DB9DD5F25BE2CB8BB.PDF *Cryptocurrencies – An assessment, Speech delivered by T. Rabi Sankar, Deputy Governor, Reserve Bank of India at Indian Banks Association 17th Annual Banking Technology Conference and Awards on February 14, 2022,* accessed on May 31, 2022

261 Kiff, John, et.al., (2020) *A Survey of Research on Retail Central Bank Digital Currency, IMF Working Paper WP/20/104,* p.9

262 https://rbidocs.rbi.org.in/rdocs//PublicationReport/Pdfs/CONCEPTNOTEACB531172E0B4DFC9A6E506C2C24FFB6.PDF *Concept Note on Central Bank Digital Currency, FinTech Department, Reserve Bank of India, October 2022,* p.15, accessed on November 1, 2022

263 *Ibid.*, p.18

264 https://www.pwc.in/assets/pdfs/consulting/financial-services/fintech/point-of-view/pov-downloads/central-bank-digital-currency-in-the-indian-context.pdf *Central Bank Digital Currency in the Indian Context, PricewaterhouseCoopers Private Limited,* p.5, accessed on July 1, 2022

265 https://www.bis.org/about/bisih/topics/cbdc.htm *BIS Innovation Hub Work on Central Bank Digital Currency (CBDC),* accessed on July 1, 2022

266 https://www.indiabudget.gov.in/doc/budget_speech.pdf *Budget 2022-23 Speech of Nirmala Sitharaman, Minister of Finance*, February 1, 2022, p.19, accessed on July 5, 2022

267 Reserve Bank of India (2022) *Press Release: 2022-23/1012, October 7*

268 Reserve Bank of India (2022) *Annual Report 2021-22,* p.12

269 https://www.rbi.org.in/Scripts/BS_SpeechesView.aspx?Id=1327 *Fintech as a Force Multiplier – Speech by Shaktikanta Das on September 22, 2022 at Mumbai,* accessed on September 28, 2022

270 Reserve Bank of India (2022) *Press Release 2022-23/1118,* October 31

271 Reserve Bank of India (2022) *Press Release 2022-23/1275,* November 29

272 https://rbidocs.rbi.org.in/rdocs//PublicationReport/Pdfs/CONCEPTNOTEACB531172E0B4DFC9A6E506C2C24FFB6.PDF *Concept Note on Central Bank Digital Currency, FinTech Department, Reserve Bank of India, October 2022,* p.6, accessed on November 1, 2022

273 https://rbidocs.rbi.org.in/rdocs/content/pdfs/71073.pdf, *Reserve Bank of India, General Administration Manual, p.14-15,* accessed on March 1, 2022

274 https://dea.gov.in/allocation-business, *Department of Economic Affairs, Ministry of Finance, Allocation of Business, p.27-28,* accessed on January 10, 2023

275 Reserve Bank of India, *Press Release, 2017-2018/1144, Nov 8, 2016*

276 Reserve Bank of India, *Press Release, 2017-2018/1146, Nov 8, 2016*

277 Reserve Bank of India, *Press Release, 2017-2018/529, Aug 24, 2017*

278 Reserve Bank of India, *Press Release, 2018-2019/174, Jul 19, 2018*

279 Reserve Bank of India, *Press Release, 2017-2018/481, Aug 18, 2017*

280 Reserve Bank of India, *Press Release, 2018-2019/2555, Apr 26, 2019*

281 Reserve Bank of India, *Press Release, 2017-2018/1848, Jan 5, 2018*

282 https://rbidocs.rbi.org.in/rdocs//PublicationReport/Pdfs/CONCEPTNOTEACB531172E0B4DFC9A6E506C2C24FFB6.PDF *Concept Note on Central Bank Digital Currency, FinTech Department, Reserve Bank of India, October 2022,* Chapter 8 p.48-49, accessed on December 1, 2022

www.ingramcontent.com/pod-product-compliance
Lightning Source LLC
LaVergne TN
LVHW070843160826
845684LV00008B/64

9798896105817